Exercises F

Brain and M

**70 Neurobic Exercises & Fun Puzzles To
Increase Mental Fitness & Boost Your Brain Juice Today
With Crossword Puzzles**

By: Jason Scotts

TABLE OF CONTENTS

PUBLISHERS NOTES

Paperback Edition

Manufactured in the United States of America

DEDICATION

This book is dedicated to individuals looking to enhance their brain and memory through fun activities.

CHAPTER 1- WHAT ARE NEUROBIC EXERCISES

A growing new body of knowledge called Neurobics is gaining popularity. Neurobics refers to mental exercises that enhance the brain's performance. Dr. Lawrence Katz was an early pioneer in the field and coined the term Neurobics. It covers a broad spectrum, drawing on some previously known ideas then adding supplemental activities to the core research.

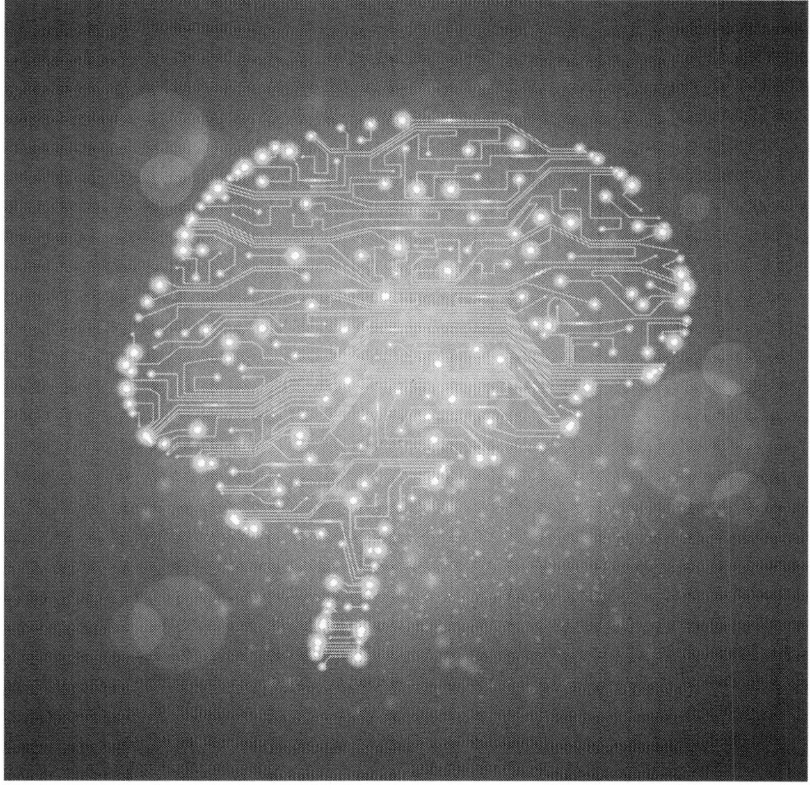

This new research in brain activity is that the brain like other parts of the body produces new cells that adapt and become integrated in the brain's overall function. Previously, it was believed that brain cells were fixed, that you had a given number at birth. Then the research branched out into producing specific activities that stimulate brain activity.

The first part of this discussion covers the background activities that stimulate brain function, starting with diet and exercise then we discuss the more complex theories of mental activity. Included here will be specific brain related exercises.

Diet

Water is the key to life. A baby in the womb is 90% water. After birth it is 80% water. As an adult we are 70% water. In old age water drops to 60%, then to 50% in death. Our brains are 75% to 90% water. As you can clearly see water is critical. The oxygen in water travels to every cell in our body. Dehydration or lack of water causes fatigue and diminishes our ability to focus and concentrate.

Some foods are especially good for us. Eating fish two or three times a week provides Omega 3. Some research indicates that it lowers dementia and strokes. Most berries especially blueberries are also beneficial.

Walnuts calm inflammation of cell walls. Raw cocoa and dark chocolate are two known antioxidants. Use baking cocoa in milk. The milk has lactose that is a form of sugar and sweetens the cocoa.

Exercise

Physical movement stimulates the brain. Playing all kinds of sports activates brain activity. Your brain processes hundreds of connections for you to perform a given sport. Dance is another activity that increases brain function.

Now we examine the mind and the brain. We often confuse the mind with the brain. The mind is non-physical while the brain is a physical organ inside our bodies. How the mind works is still a mystery. We do know that the mind processes hundreds to thoughts and sends them to the brain. Obviously the more times a thought is sent to the brain the more powerful the brain's activity will be; this is how habits are formed. The brain automatically sends signals for you to act in a certain way. On a much deeper level these habits become beliefs and control our behavior. What Neurobics does is change the thought that you send to your brain forcing it to expand and adapt to a different pattern. A study of jugglers showed that brain wave activity expanded when juggling.

We can draw upon some older techniques as well. Meditation is one such activity. Researchers have identified four levels of brain wave activity from highly active down to sleep. They are beta for very active, then alpha which is slower, followed by theta that is even slower then delta which is sleep. During meditation your brain wave activity slows going into alpha and even theta. Slower brain waves keep out extraneous thoughts. This allows the two halves of your brain to function as one. Most of our daily activity is in the active state of beta that is left brained. By moving into alpha and theta we allow the right half of our brain to activate. The right brain is the seat of intuition and creativity.

The activities of Neurobics are designed to stimulate the right brain. If we look at creativity for a moment we find that given an activity we can change the sequence, we can add parts to it or we can subtract parts from it. If we take puzzles for example, the writer has already scrambled the parts and we are to put them back into their proper order. Some Neurobic activities involve removing one of the senses such as taking a shower with our eyes closed, or turning off the lights and trying to move about by touch. Some involve the use of special scents. For sleeping for example, lavender is often used. Then you can try brushing your teeth with your non-dominant hand. What each of these exercises does is change the signals that are sent to the brain forcing you to change your behavior.

Let's take memory. Say you have a list of items you need to get from the supermarket. By making wild, off the wall associations, you'll be able to remember them better. For example, if one of the items is cabbage, you might visualize you old Aunt Alice with a big cabbage in place of her head. Studies show that the more bizarre the associations the easier it will be to remember them.

Stress

Stress causes lapses in concentration and judgment. It can affect your decision making process, memory and concentration. Here again use your creativity. Examine your daily activities and eliminate as many non- essential ones as possible. Learn to say no when you feel overburdened by others' requests.

You can use this brief summary to analyze your own behavior and find Neurobics changes that will stimulate your brain. You will recognize your brain's function as central to your overall health.

Chapter 2- Benefits of Neurobic Exercises

The brain is one of the most vital and important parts of the human body. Keeping it in shape is extremely important for people who hope to live long lives. Through the years there has been a large amount of research conducted on the brain itself. The research has provided insight into ways to improve the functionality of the brain and create better productivity and higher levels of functionality. There are many medically backed exercises and routines called "neurobic exercises" that help to improve the longevity of the brain itself, allowing it to function on a higher level as a person ages.

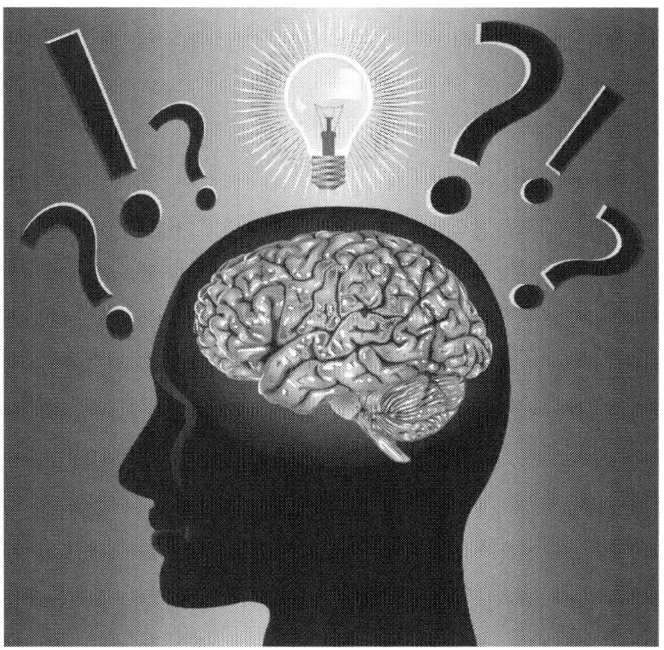

What are the benefits of neurobic exercises? Medical research suggests that by participating in a regular neurobic routine, people can improve the functionality of their brain so that it is able to take on more difficult tasks. Neurobic exercises provide a way for people to improve their brain activity and better themselves in the long run. Research also suggests that by participating in this type of exercise, people may possibly reduce their chances of Alzheimer disease or other brain affecting diseases and disorders. By utilizing a specialized routine, the overall health of the brain itself can be improved so that it is functioning at a high capacity. The brain is one of the most important parts of a body and is highly complex. The benefits of taking care of it are on par and even more important that taking care of simpler parts of the body.

Neurobic exercises are perhaps some of the best exercises to partake in, simply because they are easy to do and do not require a great set of tools or knowledge to complete. People simply focus on a set of problems or tasks specially designed to strengthen the brain. Understanding neural impulses can be a very difficult and complicated feat, but exercise through planned puzzles and thought challenges can provide an easy way in which to strengthen the brain through regular mind exercises. Planned exercises provide an easy way for people to enter their minds and improve their performances on tasks so as to be better at them in the future.

The best way to describe how these exercises work is to compare the brain to the body of an athlete. Through regular training and performance, the athlete improves. The brain itself acts the same way with neurobic exercises. The training put in to think and to use the brain allows the brain to improve and function at a much higher level. The use of these exercises and routines creates a routine for the brain to function on that allows it to improve on its everyday functionality and go forth accomplishing tasks at an improved rate. The brain is the primary learning device within the human body and utilizes many different techniques in which to take on and store further information. By improving these techniques, people are able to more readily use their brain and allow it to be strengthened as a part of the body itself.

Maintenance of the brain is important. There is a great number of deteriorating brain disorders that affect people. Exercising improves the overall functionality of not only the brain but the whole body itself. Through neurobic exercises people strengthen the brain. Bear in mind that all of the muscles are controlled through neural synapses that trigger electronic signals throughout the body. These synapses are responsible for controlling muscles that are usually strengthened through weights and training, but through neurobic exercises even greater health and control can be imposed on these muscles simply by improving the brain itself. The muscles of the body are improved when the brain is improved and thus are an integral part of having a healthy system.

Those that are seeking to live a healthy life need look no further than neurobic exercises. These exercises are a must to allow the brain to function efficiently and stave off any sort of loss of functionality or onset of diseases. It is medically proven that people who partake in these exercises are able to improve their overall health and thought process, thus allowing better functionality on a regular basis. The brain is a big organ and allows people to continue to think and to function over a long period of time. Maintaining its functionality is a must.

Enrolling in an exercise program that utilizes neurobic exercise is a step towards a healthier lifestyle. People who utilize this form of exercise are able to live a more healthy life that thus allows them to continue to function on a much grander level. Utilizing neurobic exercise is an easy way in which to move forward with a conscious plan to help the brain to function in the long run and be able to think on a much larger scale. Neurobic exercise is a must for people who care about the strength and importance of their brain. It allows better functionality and a much higher level of brain usage to be taken. Those that use neurobic exercise are thus strengthening their lives for the better.

Neurobic exercise is a must for people who care about the strength and importance of their brain. It allows better functionality and a much higher level of brain usage to be taken. Those that use neurobic exercise are thus strengthening their lives for the better.

CHAPTER 3- WHEN TO DO NEUROBIC EXERCISES

Keeping your brain strong and your memory intact should be a goal that everyone should strive for. As we age, our brains start to weaken, making us more susceptible to certain diseases of the mind. No one that I know wants to lose their memories, precious memories especially, like the day your children were born, your days in school having fun or old friends long gone. Luckily the brain can be exercised, and everyone should be challenged to do so every day.

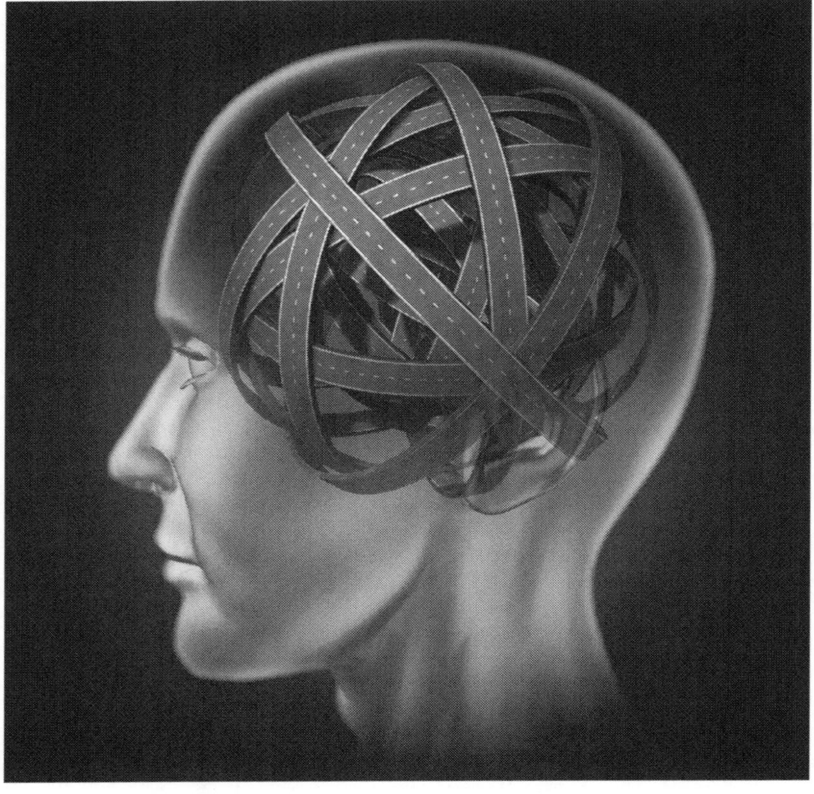

But how do we exercise our brain exactly? There are many tried and true ways, but the most common, and most fun by far, are with brain and memory games. Brain and memory games come in all different types, at varying levels of difficulty. The most common games that help strengthen the mind are puzzles. Crossword puzzles, for example, force the brain to use its cognitive powers daily to help figure the answers that go in the correct boxes. This simple exercise for the brain helps stave off neurodegenerative diseases, like Alzheimer's disease. Games like, Sudoku, also provide our brains with much needed cognitive exercise.

In this day and age, where everybody seems to have either a computer at home or a Smartphone in their pockets, there are many other ways to exercise the brain with games daily. Simple games, like Tetris, take a ton of hand to eye coordination. It also makes you think forward, where to place your next piece, which way that piece needs to fit when it gets to its destination, and then we repeat the process again.

Some of us even go as far as looking past our current piece and on to the next one in line, planning where it will go even before you have dropped or rotated the current piece. This exercise seems pointless, but put that into perspective for either a teenager or elderly adult, both of who want to drive. Being able to look forward and planning your moves and planning your routes is very important abilities that we all need to use while driving, and games like Tetris helps keep our brains sharp in this aspect.

Researchers and game designers at UCSF have built a special video game just for older adults. NeuroRacer is a great example of the importance of playing games for the brain. These researchers found that the adults that were playing their game strengthened their multi-tasking cognitive skills, which helped to not only remedy certain targeted brain deficiencies, but also helped strengthen their working memory. The working memory is the part of the brain that allows us to remember simple things, like a person's name that they have just given us, or their email address. In some cases, the older adults were on par with the cognitive multi-tasking skills of a much younger person. Simple steps forward like this for some people are very important, especially in the early stages of mental a disease, and even old age itself.

For the younger generation of people out there, these games still have great value in strengthening the brain and memory. Some students have problems maintaining information that they need, important details and facts that may seem to slip away from them when it comes time to test them. By playing certain mind strengthening games, that student can train their brain to hold more information than they has previously, and for longer periods of time. It also helps them maintain better focus in the classroom; this in turn gives them the chance to absorb more information. Even young toddlers and children need memory games.

The game Memory is a perfect example of a memory training game, and can be used for young children, all the way through to the elderly. The premise of the game is simple, use your memory to remember where each card is, and try to find matching pairs while remembering the layout. It seems simple enough, and it is. But do not underestimate the power of this useful game, for even the parents of young children who are playing with them can still, and often do, make mistakes. It is imperative that we not let our brains become lax and useless tools that sit on the shelf and gather dust.

What happens when we forget to exercise our leg and arm muscles? They grow soft and weak, unable to lift the heavier objects as easily as someone who keeps in shape. They start to have problems holding our bodies up us as well, making it difficult to walk, or even stand up straight. The same thing can happen to our brains if we do not exercise them regularly. The connections in our brain that help with our cognitive skills get soft, and some even fade away completely. This cerebral atrophy is common in many aging adults, and even more common in adults that are suffering from dementia and Alzheimer's. By playing these games, these puzzles and challenges, we are exercising our brains in much the same way as we would exercise our muscles.

There are many other simple exercises and games that we can use to keep our minds sharp. Using and reading an analog watch, for example, can have the same positive effects on your brain and as a puzzle game. Even games like Blackjack can have an effect on the brain, and other similar games, that encourage the use of math and memory to try to predict the best move each round. There are also complex mind puzzles that have you using your brain and fingers to try to undo pieces of the puzzle, using trial and error to find the solution to each complex problem.

But no matter what your chosen brain or memory game is, just remember that just having the puzzles and games around is not enough to take advantage of their benefits. That is the same as having a home gym that you never use. You must use them regularly on a daily basis, training your memory, strengthening your other cognitive skills, and having fun while doing it. It does not matter if you are a 2 year old with a memory game, a 35 year old with a crossword puzzle, or a 75 year old with a special designed video game, we all need to make sure that we are keeping our minds strong and sharp.

Chapter 4- When To Do Neurobic Exercises

Most people have heard the expression that the brain needs to be worked like a muscle. That makes sense, it is one of the most important organs in your body, you use it for nearly every activity, cerebral or otherwise, but where can you actually workout your brain? Schooling and education help, but it doesn't fully engage your brain. To have the brain fully engaged, you want to engage all the neurons, from the ones that help you think, to the ones that help you brush your teeth. While you can't take your brain to your local gym to do brain squats, there are neurobic exercises that can help.

What are Neurobic Exercises?

Neurobic exercises involve getting your brain out of its comfort zone by exposing it to new sensations or challenges that are out of the routine. An example would be to cook with your other hand, or even buying a new air freshener than you usually use. There are three basic types of these exercises.

Physical

This involves changing some kind of action that you normally do, or exposing your body to new physical challenges or situations that involve not only the muscles working differently, but changing how the brain thinks of the body. A simple exercise in this domain is switching hands every twenty seconds while brushing. First count up to twenty, and then down to twenty to add a little bit of mental Neurobics to that as well. For more intensive physical neurobic practice, consider an activity like Pilates or yoga.

Mental and Emotional

This involves changing the way you think or feel about something. Mental Neurobics can involve counting, checking ones memory with little games, trying to think in a foreign language, and so much more. Here the point is not to test your brain in something you are already good at, but rather to expose your brain to something that you perhaps have never done before, and let your brain try its best to solve the new situation. More intensive training in this domain can be achieved with video games, Sudoku, and Luminosity training.

Sensational

This might be the most fun, but least expected of all the exercises. This involves switching up the things you feel, taste, smell, hear, and see. This is also the broadest category as changing up the poster scheme in your room or workshop is a neurobic exercises. Another fun exercise is to change the temperature of the water for you shower or bath every couple of days.

Best Time for Regular Practice

For the average person, two great times to practice neurobic exercises, in the morning and before you go to sleep.

In the morning, you are required to do so many early morning tasks that require movement. By varying up your routine, you help challenge your brain to grow and be more adaptive. When brushing your teeth, try switching hands; use a different temperature of water than you usually do in the shower. The whole point is to vary up your actions and sensations to give your brain something new to be exposed to every day.

Before you go to bed is the other time that is best to do some neurobic exercises. Besides a little bit of physical exercises with brushing teeth, maybe changing up the routine in which one puts on their pajamas, this is the perfect time for mental exercises. You can take advantage of the hypnagogic period, which is where your body is falling asleep and you have greater access to the depths of your brain. While in this state try everything from mental math, visualization, and meditation. Try to find a routine, something that feels comfortable to you. Practice that routine for two weeks, then change it. The whole point of neurobic exercises is to force you out of your comfort zone, remember?

Good Instances to use Neurobic Exercises

The most appropriate time to work on your Neurobic exercises will be dependent on your lifestyle. Students would benefit from mental neurobic exercises both upon waking and before sleeping, but they would get an extra edge if they practice mental math or speaking in a foreign language in their head for ten minutes before an exam.

Athletes and skilled labor have the most to gain from physical exercises. Doing some physical Neurobics such as varying the morning and nightly routines are a great way to start. However to gain the utmost benefit, the individual should take a class such as yoga for two week, then change it for a cardiovascular exercise class. By changing the routine and being exposed to so many athletic disciplines, the body and the brain controlling the body become ready for anything.

Sensational Neurobics are applicable to everyone. By creating sensational plasticity, the brain becomes able to deal with a wider variety of feelings, including stress and pain. It may seem ironic, but by alternating warm, scented baths with those of ice water, a person actually becomes emotionally stronger.

The Golden Years

Besides turmeric root, there is nothing better for the brain than neurobic exercises. During the golden years, it is advised to practice this anywhere between 3-5 times per day. This can help keep the mind agile and prevent or slow the progression of Alzheimer's disease.

CHAPTER 5- CHOOSING NEUROBIC EXERCISES

Not all Neurobic exercises are created equal. Just like in fitness you have exercises that work for most people and those that don't work for anyone at all. Through trial and error we find what works best for us and we stick with it. The same applies to neurobic exercises. There are practices that are put out there that have gotten rave reviews and those that have fallen by the wayside never to be mentioned again. You might be asking yourself, "Well what separates an exercise an exercise that's just good from one that is the best?" The answer to that question is simple. It depends on the person.

There are certain things you should look for in a good neurobic exercise. The signs that a neurobic exercise is good are if it grabs your attention, uses more than one of your senses and breaks routines that a person you are used to. Deciding what exercises are the best is a little bit harder than that. What is the best for one person might not be the best for another person.

There a hundreds of neurobic exercises out there. You have to choose what would benefit you in the longer run and improve what you are already doing. A baseball player will benefit more from a practice that improves his hand-eye coordination than one that improves his sense of smell. A cook will benefit from a practice what improves his sense of smell than one that improves his hand-eye coordination. Different exercises work for different types of people.

In the next few paragraphs I will explain how to find out which practices are best for you.

The first thing you should ask yourself before choosing an exercise is if it will improve your quality of life. A good exercise should improve upon what you're doing already. If you are a person who works in the manufacturing industry a neurobic exercise that improves your focus and reflexes might help you. If you are someone who loves to read a lot an exercise that improves your memory might be the best for you. You have to decide what you are trying to accomplish and choose what exercises will help you reach those goals. Examine your weaknesses. If you are someone who becomes too stuck in routines you will need to choose an exercise that helps you to break the monotony. Evaluate your weaknesses then move forward from there.

The next thing you should ask yourself when choosing an exercise is how convenient it is. Will you have to set aside ten minutes just to do it or is it something you can do quickly? Depending on your lifestyle, a shorter exercise might suit you better. If you are a person who has a lot of time on their hands then you have plenty more options to work with. Evaluate your activities for the day and pick out the best time to fit in an exercise.

Another question to ask is "Will this exercise inconvenience me in any way? There is a neurobic exercise that gives the suggestion to take a new route to work as a way to break up old routines. If there are only two routes to work and the only alternate route is always backed up with traffic then I don't think that exercise would be the best for you.

Something important that you should factor in is if there's scientific research behind the exercise. You should do things based on how they make you feel but you have to know how exercises are affecting you physically if you're going to be doing them on a daily basis. You never want to jump into something blindly. That applies to anything in life. You should research the exercise on the internet or at the library and read reviews for the exercises. If you are getting the exercise from a book read the literary sources. Read about the science behind Neurobics. Knowing the science behind what you are practicing factors a lot into picking the best exercise for yourself.

The final factor that will help you pick the best exercise is choosing where you are actually getting the exercise from. You have to make sure that you get the exercise from a trusted source. The source not only has to be trusted but they must give the proper instructions. Without the proper instructions what you are supposed to experience when doing an exercise might not come to fruition. The internet has a lot of articles on neurobic exercises. This is a good and a bad thing. The good thing is that many more people will find out about neurobic exercises and gain benefits from doing them. The bad thing is that the more something is spread around the more the original instructions become watered down.

Now that I have discussed the criteria for choosing the best exercise I hope that you will make good use of it. Choose your exercises wisely. Take your time and do your research. When the right exercise comes along you will definitely know it.

CHAPTER 6- 24 BASIC NEUROBIC EXERCISES

These mental workouts increase your synaptic connections with multi-sensory experience. Remember, anything that breaks your daily routine can be stimulating.

Smell Your Spices

Get a pen and paper and put all your spices on a table. Blindfold yourself and take one jar or bottle of spices and smell deeply. Try to identify which spice it is by smell or touch. Write down the spices name while still blindfolded. Like "#1 oregano" on your paper and set the bottles in a single row. When you inhale the last spice remove your blindfold to see how accurate you were.

Draw a Picture of Something without Looking At It

Put several small items in a box and pick one without looking. Use your fingers to get an idea of the lines and contours. Picture it in your head and draw it with a pen without opening your eyes. For an added challenge use crayons or markers to imagine it's color too.

Play With Glass

Gather assorted glass containers around the house. Fill them each with the same amount of water. Tap each one to produce vibrations and listen for the differences in tone or pitch from each glass. Experiment with different amounts of water or tapping with different objects (your finger, a toothpick, feathers, etc). Try to focus on your sense of touch as much as your sense of hearing. Use your vision to see the shapes of the glasses and their features. Observe any changes in the glasses like refraction or rainbows.

Use Your Non-Dominant Hand

Try an exercise like brushing your hair or teeth. Try writing with your opposite hand or tying your shoes. You can try doing things one handed or do not use your thumbs. Get creative. Be safe and do not do this for activities like driving or chopping with a knife.

Mute the T.V.

Turn the sound down on your television and use the subtitles. Try using the foreign language subtitles. You may be surprised how much you can infer from visual context alone.

What's for Dinner?

While eating dinner try naming a different fact about each bite. Make a note of the texture, weight in grams or ounces, or a fact about the food's appearance or flavor. This stimulates neuron connections because although people eat, they do not use their powers of perception while doing so.

Word Puzzles

Games like crossword puzzles, Scrabble™ or find a word puzzles all contribute to word recall and you may learn some new words to expand your vocabulary. Try to concentrate on the shape of the letters as you read or spell them out. Note any special fonts or mistakes in the printing as you go along. Touch the paper or game piece to absorb more than just what is written on it.

Clothes

Wear clothing with textures. Wear your clothes inside out or backwards. If possible wear pajamas during the day and casual clothes at night for a week. If you are able, wear shoes on your hands or as a hat. Necklaces make good belts, ties are excellent bracelets and hats can become purses.

Breakfast and Lunch

Switch the menu for breakfast to foods you normally eat at lunch like hamburgers. Top this with some of every condiment you can think of. Instead of a bun, try a tortilla, cornbread, bagel or pita. Do not just taste the different items; look at the food color and the new unusual textures. How does this new breakfast smell or feel in your hands? For lunch, make pancakes or have bacon and eggs. Sit on the table or floor. Eat from a large serving platter or a fancy glass. Eat with chop sticks.

Speak in all quotes for one hour or one day

This may require some research beforehand but is quite effective in the long run.

Operate according to a different time zone.

Make a non-rubber band ball.

Collect stretchy materials and layer it on a ball as you would a rubber band ball. As you layer each item test its elasticity and how it sounds as you pluck it. Visually observe any changes in the material as you stretch it.

This should give you an idea of how to proceed with your changes in the standard routine. Some other changes to attempt for the improvement of your neural pathways are the following.

Take the long way to your destinations.

Move your furniture around at home or work.

Change the font of all documents you are typing to something new when appropriate.

Wear your hair in a different style.

Use candlelight.

Listen to a new type of music or instrument.

Study for a test unrelated to your education or vocation.

Watch the local news for a far away city or other place.

Make a meal from your kitchen based on memory and smell.

Turn off all lights in your home and go by touch and sound.

Close your eyes and pick out your clothes by touch alone.

Try to find something based on your sense of touch using a body part other than your hands (elbow or nose).

Chapter 7- Speed Exercises

Speed reading is a valuable skill that many people utilize to double the words per minute that they read from an average of two hundred fifty words per minute to an average of five hundred words per minute. It can be an asset for those who often have to read lengthy documents or policy for their careers as it provides them with additional time for other tasks and helps them view the big picture of the content that they read. Here are ten exercises to help you learn to speed read and the reasons why each one is effective.

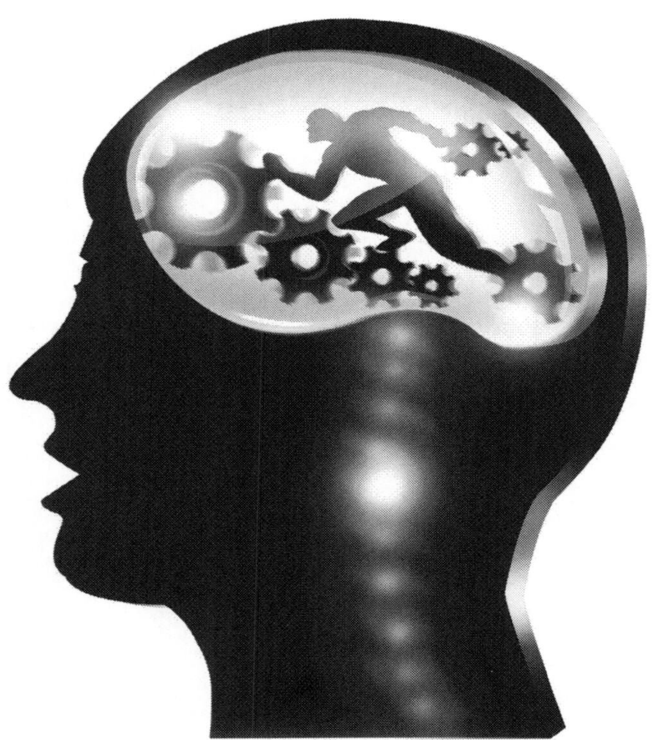

Learn to Chunk Words: Chunking is a process that entails looking at groups of words rather than just reading one word at a time. Most people already utilize this skill to an extent but it is important to take note of how many words you currently chunk then try to increase that number. This process helps you speed read because it eliminates time that is wasted focusing on individual words and rather puts the emphasis on groups of words or chunks.

Train Your Eyes: Eyes are able to look at and focus on just over one and a half inches of a line of text but the majority of people who read do not use this to their advantage. Use a ruler while reading to take note of how much space on the page you actually look at while reading and try to view an entire one and a half inches of space. This is a beneficial exercise because it trains the eye to move quickly and see more of the content.

Practice in the Morning: When training yourself to speed read, be sure to practice in the morning as much as possible. The reason that this is important is that studies have shown our brains are better able to concentrate and focus in the mornings. Once you have become a successful speed reader you will be able to read at any time of day but while in the learning stages, mornings are ideal.

Use a Prop: A variety of props can be helpful when learning to speed read. For example, a pointer of some sort such as a pen or pencil will help guide the eyes. This forces the eyes to keep up with the brain and in turn makes speed reading possible. Another helpful prop is an index card or piece of paper to keep the eyes focused on one line while quickly dragging it down the page. This again ensures that the eyes keep up with the brain to become an effective speed reader.

Keep Track of Progress: Another important exercise when learning to speed read is tracking progress. This is because it is hard to know whether you have increased your words per minute speed without keeping an accurate record of where you started and where you ended. Setting goals is a proven way to motivate one to increase their dedication to learning a new task.

Improve Your Concentration: Concentration is vital when learning to speed read. Improve your concentration by removing all external distractions and avoiding multi-tasking.

Internal distractions may also be a problem if you are unable to focus on the material. Improving concentration is an effective exercise because speed readers often lack the ability to comprehend material when they are not focused or have not practiced speed reading techniques often enough to eliminate both internal and external distractions.

Avoid Regression: Regression is something that many speed readers do when they first begin to speed read. It is when you "miss" a word then go back to reread that word. It is important to train your eyes and your brain to simply skip the word instead of regress back to read it. Overall understanding can still easily be reached even if you miss an occasional word while reading. Regression is a waste of time so it is vital to avoid while learning to speed read.

Skim or Preview: Skimming or previewing the material prior to reading is an effective speed reading exercise. This is because it provides the reader with an overview of the big picture so they are not as focused on the word for word details as they might be if they did not skim the material first. Take a look at large headings and opening sentences as a way to increase comprehension and improve your reading speed.

Keep Your Mouth Closed: A lot of people read words out loud or mouth the words without intending to do so. This is hugely detrimental to speed readers because it trains the brain to focus on just one word at a time rather than chunking the words as discussed in the first tip. While reading, make a point to keep your mouth shut at all times so you are not tempted to mouth the words or read them out loud.

Do Not Highlight or Take Notes: It may seem quite obvious that highlighting and note taking are not components of speed reading but a lot of people make the mistake of using these tools. If a reading task requires either one of these components then it is not a task for speed reading. Highlighting and taking notes distract the reader which makes it more difficult for them to focus on the aforementioned techniques.

Most of us read quite a bit each and every day. We may read e-mails or reports at work, books and magazines for pleasure at home, and a wide variety of signs, memos, and posts throughout the average day. Keeping this in mind, speed reading can be a cherished skill to possess. Practice the ten aforementioned exercises over and over again as a way to increase your reading speed as well as your overall comprehension of the text. This is a skill that can be used by many people in many different professions but it requires extensive practice and willingness to learn.

Chapter 8- 24 Exercises To Enhance The Senses

It is too easy to become stuck in a rut when your daily routine becomes redundant. Therefore, it is important to try and implement new and challenging tasks into your everyday life, ensuring that you never grow stagnate in life. Here are 24 neurobic exercises to engage your senses while also stimulating your mind.

Get dressed with your eyes closed.

Anytime you perform an activity while stripping yourself of a vital sense, it heightens the other senses. Although closing your eyes while getting dressed blocks your sense of sight, it will heighten your sense of touch, along with mental vision.

Take a new route on your way to work in the morning.

As trivial as it may seem, the path you take on your way to work or school each morning has a great effect on your mood for the rest of the day. Taking a typical route each day will set the course for a boring and all too familiar routine. However, when you take an alternate route, you are stimulating your mind since it is unfamiliar with its surroundings and is forced to work harder in order to comprehend the new route.

Listen to a piece of music while smelling an aroma.

The music will excite your sense of hearing while the aroma—be it a flower, scented candle, or incense—will arouse your sense of smell. When the two combine, it enhances your inner vision.

Rearrange your living space and/or work space.

Similar to changing the route you take to work or school each morning, our mind becomes overly familiar with our immediate surroundings, as it should by nature. Therefore, it is up to us to find ways to keep ourselves constantly motivated mentally. An act as simple as rearranging the furniture in your living room, or the materials you get on your work desk force our brain to reconsider everything around us, no matter how mundane it may seem on the surface.

Purchase food from a farmer's market versus a supermarket.

Do not engage in any social networking activity for a full week.

As important as social networking is in this digital age, it lacks the same mental stimulus that you receive when communicating with someone in purpose. Taking a mere week off will force you to interact with friends, family, as well as perfect strangers on a more intimate level.

Do not watch any television for a full week.

If giving up your usage of social networking is not enough, why not try giving up television as well? For some people, this may be easier than the former.

Eat outside as opposed to inside.

Eating outside versus in a closed off environment automatically stimulates your sensory system.

Walk backwards.

If the idea of walking backwards in public is too much for you, then just it out in the privacy of your own home. Even then, your mind will have to work twice as hard as usual to comprehend this subtle change in the environment properly.

Start keeping a journal.

Each morning, write for thirty minutes. Whether you keep your journal on your computer or through the more traditional media of a notepad, it is essential that you write from the heart, as opposed to the mind, meaning don't think about what you are writing; just write.

If you are a smoker, stop smoking.

The only thing more addictive to a smoker than nicotine is routine. The smoker is drawn to the familiarity of it all. If they typically smoke while driving, then they will feel compelled to light up a cigarette each time they get behind the wheel of their car.

Move around more (jogging/walking/hiking).

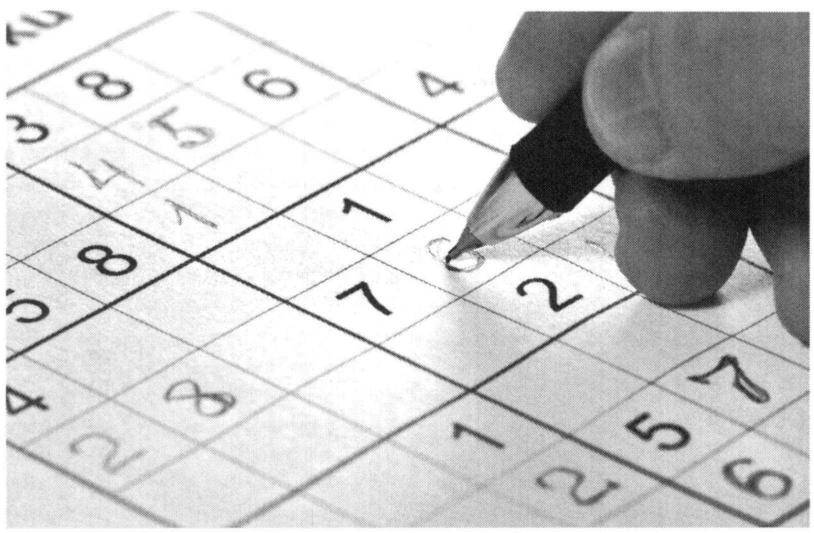

Complete a crossword and/or Sudoku puzzle each morning.

Learn how to play chess.

Try some new (foreign) foods.

If possible, see if there are any food festivals happening near you. This is the perfect opportunity to indulge in unfamiliar foods and maybe even find something you like.

Change your eating habits.

Poor dietary habits can put us into a rut. Incorporating healthier foods (fruits, vegetables, and other non-processed foods) into your diet is a surefire way to emerge from whatever slump you may find yourself in.

Communicate non-verbally for a day.

If you are able to make it for a day, then go ahead and aim for an entire week of non-verbal communication with others.

Listen to music while you eat.

Rearrange your morning routine.

If the first thing you do each morning is wash your face, then don't. Instead, take the time after you step out of bed to perform small exercises.

Use your other hand for executing everyday tasks.

Complete other everyday tasks with your eyes closed.

Watch the clouds while you play with a ball of clay.

Drive somewhere with no set agenda.

The mental freedom will allow you to notice places you may have not otherwise noticed had you been set on going somewhere specifically.

Learn a new language.

Chapter 9- 22 Exercises To Combine The Senses

It has become evident that exercise for the brain plays as important a role in our daily lives as does exercise for the body. Most enthusiasts think nothing of joining a gym or adding things such as jogging and walking to their daily routine. Along with proper diet and activities such as these, people feel they are doing all they can to promote good health within themselves. Oddly enough, there are very few that realize brain fitness is as vital to health as body workout programs.

From the day we are born, the human brain is a magnet for all the new information that is being fed to it. While an infant explores the world around them, each sound, color, and learned activity, continues to promote the health of the brain. This process continues throughout our lives but it is the learning years in particular that do the most to stimulate the neural network. There are thousands upon thousands of neurons in the human brain and each one of them is linked with the others to enhance our ability to think and learn.

As we age, many become complacent as to what is needed to engage ourselves in neurobic exercise. Despite what we do in daily life, things become more and more repetitive until the skills we gained so easily between the infant and young adult years are lost. Often without realizing it, the same things are done day in and day out.

The brain of an adult weighs approximately three pounds. For a bodily organ weighing so little it is awe inspiring when one takes the time to realize that without it the body would cease to exist. Neurons not only continually transmit signals to one another, they are the catalyst that prompts our lungs to breathe; our heart to beat; and the controlling factor of every move we make. Without neurons we could not run, walk, or lift weights to keep the body in shape. They allow us flight when in danger and transmit pain when something in the body is amiss.

It has been proven without doubt that neurobic exercise does far more than any other kind we can indulge in. Without it, none of the other things we take for granted are possible. Diseases such as dementia and Alzheimer's have been shown to be prevented simply by using neurobic exercise and yet we see so many of our elderly suffering from these maladies. These are ailments that could have been prevented entirely or at least kept so minimal that people could continue to live productive lives.

Perhaps you are beginning to wonder how this form of exercise works. The answer is quite simple. Use any form of stimuli you can think of that will keep your neurons functioning in a healthy manner. The methods that can be used are all around us and so obvious that many fail to even recognize them.

What we have to do is revert to our younger years when all of life was a learning experience. As mentioned in previous chapters, if you are right handed, try using your left hand for daily activities such as using the TV remote or brushing your teeth. The use of all our senses is good for us in the long run. Try closing your eyes when performing easy tasks such as buttoning a shirt or blouse, washing your face, or trying to locate your house keys on a table. These activities will sharpen your sense of touch.

Our sense of smell can also be utilized in new ways when we awake to new and novel aromas. Find ways to replace the aroma of coffee and during the day visit places such as bakeries where odors are rich and distinctive. Try your hand at learning new games. If you have never played chess, learn. Try your hand at crossword puzzles and other forms of amusement such as Sudoku and other varieties of puzzles. Read books and newspapers with abandon. If you have some simple mathematics to figure out, use your head and forget the calculator. From time to time, change the route you take to and from work. Not only is this considered a safety feature but it is a stimulant for the brain because you are forced to think about the streets you have to take.

If you have always enjoyed sports become a participant rather than a spectator. If you have some physical problem that deters you from strenuous activity, try a less vigorous sport such as swimming. Learn a language, travel the world, and indulge in crafts or hobbies. Make new friends and socialize with them, forgo the pen and use a pencil, or listen to your favorite kind of music. When it is time for a coffee break, pass up the java and go for a fast walk instead.

Neurobic exercises are all around us in every walk of life. All we need do is seek them out. Every experience that we sense in our daily lives is an opportunity to keep our brains young. We must challenge our neurons in various novel ways as often as we can.

Chapter 10- Number Exercises For Your Brain & Memory

Numerical exercises can be very useful tools and they have been used for decades. There are several kinds of numerical exercises. These exercises are mainly used to test a person's ability and overall performance.

First, there are exercises that analyze the long term effect of physical exercise on adolescents. This exercise essentially chooses a number of children between ages 11 and 13 to analyze the benefits of exercise over a prolonged period of time. Hopefully this exercise will teach young people the importance of daily exercise and weight control.

Basically, the exercise analysis proved to have positive benefits on adolescents' psychological and mental well-being. Many adolescents and teenagers in today's society are overweight. In addition, prolonged exercise can result in higher self-esteem among a select group of adolescents. Therefore, this exercise analysis has many positive results for many people.

The Euler Method was designed to help a student find numerical solutions. This method presents the various differences between numerical quantities and how they are used and applied. The Euler Method focuses on how to reach a specific value of X. This method is useful to those who pursue a career which involves upper level mathematics as well as science. The Euler Method has been used for a number of years.

Improving Test Scores is another example of a useful numerical exercise. This exercise teaches a person that numerical reasoning can be reached only through applying specific strategies and perspectives within a timely fashion. An exercise related to helping improve test scores will challenge concentration and overall mathematical ability. Although, intelligence level normally remains the same it has been proven that test scores of certain individuals can improve over a period of time.

Finding Roots of Polynomials is an example of a numerical exercise geared toward improving a person's math ability. Essentially polynomials teach us that the real number X is always equal to a. Polynomials have linear factors that can only be found through certain numerical methods. This exercise also experiments with large polynomials and their various applications. Polynomials and their properties are considered to be upper level mathematics. However, basic applications of polynomials are now taught as part of a general mathematical curriculum.

Percentages are a good example of a numerical exercise. Percentages are taught to students as part of a basic mathematical curriculum. Percentages are helpful when attempting to find differences between various numerical quantities. Percentages also help make fractions easier to solve in some cases. Percentages are generally referred to as basic mathematics which is usually taught to students in elementary school.

Psychometric Testing are useful tools which measure a person's true mental abilities. In order to do well with a test of this nature you must prepare well in advance. A test of this nature should prepare the person to give positive, impacting and effective presentations. Psychometric testing focuses a great deal on personality traits and overall educational abilities. In addition, a great deal of time is spent on the construction of instrument as well as procedures for measurement. This exercise is also designed to sharpen a person's motor skills and ability.

Thermoluminescence Techniques are used in many dating applications as well as the analysis of TL data. Thermoluminescence is taught as part of a curriculum for students studying for a career in advanced science, research technology and medicine. Thermoluminescence is a form of Luminescence which is characterized by crystalline materials and some minerals. Applications of this nature can be quite difficult and are normally reserved for those who have demonstrated above average performance in mathematics.

Thermoluminescence has proven to be a useful tool in the analysis of sand migration. Thermoluminescence has been used extensively when studying radiation as well as its long term effects. We know today that radiation can cause cancer after prolonged exposure.

Verbal and Numerical Reasoning Exercises are helpful when recruiting new officers of the law. Many police academies use verbal and numerical reasoning tests when seeking new police recruits. This exercise can accurately access a person's overall ability to solve problems within a timely manner. In addition, exercises of this nature can easily access mental or psychological abilities. Police work is stressful and can cause depression for some officers therefore; this is an extremely useful exercise to give beforehand. This exercise is given many times in conjunction with psychological counseling.

The ability to communicate in an effective manner is critical for almost any job or profession. Verbal and numerical testing can quickly identify one's ability to effectively communicate with a person of authority. Some people have difficulty relating to a person who is in authority.

Beginner Numerical Exercises are often used to access general verbal and mathematical abilities. A beginner exercise discusses variables, data variation, numerical operations and random number generation. This exercise is very basic and it is still used widely today mainly for pre-employment screening purposes. This exercise is very similar to a numerical reasoning test. This test is considered very basic which could prove to be ideal for those who find difficulty in upper level mathematics.

Numerical Exercises in Calculus is an exercise in upper level mathematics. Calculus focuses a great deal on derivative numbers, mean value and linearization. Calculus is an advanced mathematics that is normally required for those studying for a career in science, medicine and engineering. Exercises in calculus teach the person various applications of limits and continuity, derivatives as well as definite integrals. In addition, calculus also introduces infinite numbers and mathematics pertaining to parametric vector. Mathematics of this nature can prove to be very difficult to the average person. Therefore, mathematics of this nature is normally reserved for those with a better than average math ability.

There are various numerical exercises that are still used today. These exercises were originally designed to test ones intellectual ability and mental performance. Many employers use numerical exercises as a means of choosing the best qualified for a particular job position. These exercises can include or exclude a person seeking a job within a particular industry.

Chapter 11- Word Puzzles

Imagine that each son in a family has an equal number of brothers and sisters. Each daughter has two times the number of brothers as sisters. How many daughters and sons are in the family?

John steps on a scale and weighs 120 pounds. Jane steps on the scale and weighs 100 pounds. When they step on the scale together, they weigh 210 pounds. Upon examining the scale, they found the zero point was set incorrectly. Is the reading on the scale too high or is it too low?

Two clocks are set at noon. One clock gains five minutes each hour. The other loses five minutes each hour. At what time will the two clocks show an hour difference in time?

Susan is the middle runner in a race. Danielle is in 10th place and slower than Susan. Linda is in 16th place. How many runners are in the race?

A man drives to work at an average speed of 50 miles per hour. It takes an hour and 15 minutes to arrive. Going home, he also drives at an average speed of 50 miles per hour. It takes 75 minutes. Explain how this is possible.

One container has peaches; a second has pears, and a third both peaches and pears. All of the containers have been labeled incorrectly. Is it possible to pick one piece of fruit from a container and determine the correct labels without looking inside the containers?

I am the sister of a piano player. I do not have any sisters. How is this possible?

A man fails to stop at a stop sign. Realizing he left his driver's license at home, he drives three blocks down a one-way street. Why wasn't he stopped by a policeman?

How many rotations does a penny revolve, when it is rolled around the edge of another penny lying flat on a surface?

There are 10 green and 10 red ornaments in a drawer. Without looking, how many ornaments must be taken out to be assured of having two of the same color? How many have to be taken out to assure two ornaments are different in color?

There is a great deal of controversy over a precise definition of intelligence. Individuals who score high on an IQ test may have little aptitude for matters that are defined as common sense. Simple solutions may escape them, but complex theories in science can be easily explained.

Being smart can mean possessing knowledge. To some, the lack of ability to reason and apply that knowledge is not considered smart. There are arguments that intelligence has multiple facets versus a general intelligence theory.

Brain training is meant to improve memory, attention, speed, flexibility and problem solving.

Memory builders including remembering an object's location, recalling a name after being introduced, quick and accurate learning of new subject matter, and simultaneously keeping track of more than one idea.

Attention training deals with staying focused on tasks for lengthy periods of time, improving precision and production, maintaining concentration while learning something new, and avoiding distractions.

Puzzles that have individuals monitor two information streams simultaneously are called dual n-back tests. One source of information is auditory. The other is visual. Pressing a key is required when an established target from one or both streams is presented. Attention must be split between the two output channels. Designers of these tests believe that being able to improve attention control will improve intelligence.

Improved ability to complete tasks within a set time frame has caused adjustments to be made to IQ tests. As more time is spent in formal educational settings, education becomes improved. Every 10 to 15 years IQ tests are made more difficult.

Speed concepts include making time-sensitive decisions, increasing cognitive processing, speed, making adaptations to environment changes, and quick reactions.

Improving flexibility makes it easier to communicate clearly, think outside of normal parameters, avoid making mistakes, and quickly and efficiently multi-task.

Problem Solving aspects are dissection of complex information, estimations made accurately, mental calculations, and determination of the best course of action.

Theories on improving brain function are often quickly embraced because people are looking for easy ways to improve intelligence. The brain performs more functions than creating and thinking. Motor functions like breathing, balance, and movement are also controlled by the brain. Neurons in the brain work together to absorb, process, store, and recall information. This happens unconsciously.

Reasoning test scores are thought to be improved with training. A study was conducted that had subjects watch patterns that changed down columns or across rows. An inference needed to be formulated to describe the changes. Four groups were formed. One group underwent 12 training sessions. A second group was presented with 17 sessions. The third group attended 19 training sessions. A control group had no training after the initial test. When retested, groups with training fared better than those without training. The longer training sessions produced the highest scores. The findings were proportional. More training meant better scores.

It should be noted that some researchers disputed the results. Those disputers conducted a similar battery of tests. Adjustments were in the number of tests completed initially. "No contact" returnees revealed the same results as the original test. However, the findings questioned the claim of more training yielding better scores.

Aging, without neuron growth in the hippocampus, causes the brain to deteriorate. Keeping active is believed to prevent deterioration. Enriched environments that provide stimuli from toys and games have been compared to physical exercise. Neuron growth was measured to determine results.

Testing was done with mice. Exercise provided two to six times more neurogenesis in mice versus those that did not exercise. Environmental stimuli seemed to have no effect on neuron growth. The study leads to speculation, that neurons spawned by activity, helps with memory and learning more than specific learning activities.

Regardless of theory, nearly all researchers agree that exercise for the body and exercise for the mind are equally important.

CHAPTER 12- MEMORY PUZZLES

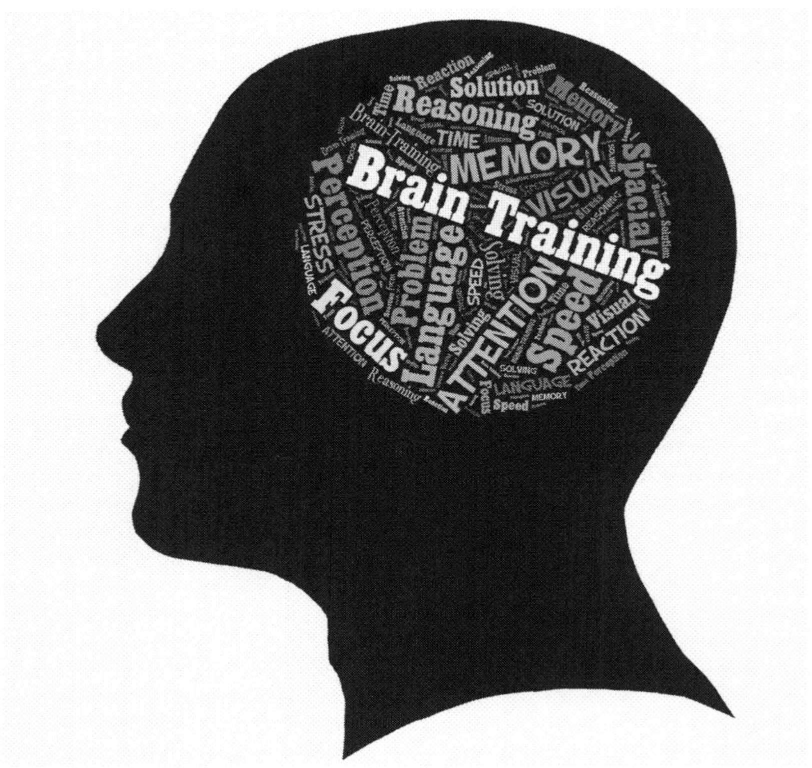

There are all sorts of different ways to stay fit, and although many of these activities focus around your body and the way it looks, it is also important for you to exercise the way your mind works as well. This is going to keep your mind healthy and prevent the signs of different mental conditions. This way, you are able to stay sharp and focused, no matter how old you are or what you do during the rest of your day.

Braid

This is a game you can play on your mobile Smartphone or tablet, and it combines both puzzle logic with that of a platform video game, so it makes it incredibly entertaining and one of the most desired brain games on a mobile device. You are going to have different tools throughout the game, and you need to figure out how to combine these items in order to progress through it. It isn't like other point and click adventure games, but it keeps your brain thinking and working through problems in order to complete it. It isn't tricky or extremely difficult. , but it does keep you on your toes.

Solitaire

This is the classic card game that, while you can play it with your own deck of cards, it might just be easier to play it on a computer or phone somewhere. This game helps you count fast and match items. It also works with your eye coordination, as you have to be able to see the matches in order to progress through the game. Whether you do one card draws or three card craws, this is an excellent game for staying sharp and passing the time.

Crossword Puzzles

You don't need a digital device to complete all these puzzles. This is an oldie but goodie. With a pencil and the crossword puzzle, you can rack your brain, and possibly the brain of your neighbor, in order to complete the task. Chances are you are going to be thinking hard and trying to determine what the clues mean, in order to answer many of these questions.

Sudoku

This number game forces your brain to look through rows of numbers, in order to make sure it does not appear in any nine number square, nine digital row, or nine digit column. There is generally only one way to win each game, and it requires you to stay on top of the game and to be continually thinking and processing the information. It keeps your brain engaged the entire time, so you really can't stop thinking about the game, or else you are going to mess up.

Portal and Portal 2

This is one of the most popular computer and video game puzzle games of all time, so if you enjoy technology and video game systems, this is an excellent option for you. In the game, you create portals into surfaces that allow you to interact with different rooms and locations. You have to create the portal accurately in order to interact with the material and items in a completely different room; otherwise the entire campaign is not going to work. This tests the logic aspect of your brain and forces you to see things that are going to happen, before it happens.

Angry Birds

Yes, while it is one of the most popular applications of all time, it is also a great way to test your brain. This is because the game uses physics in order to determine where your birds fly, especially in the "Angry Birds: Space" and "Angry Birds: Star Wars" versions. You have to alter the flight path of your bird in order to circle planets and asteroids, and if you don't do it at just the right angle, it is not going to work at all. This is a fun game for all ages, and it requires you to process all information in the game in order to be successful.

Flashcards

Flashcards basically has you place a bunch of cards face down on the ground (there are also applications for this) and you are able to flip up two cards at a time. If the cards match, you remove them, but if they don't, you have to flip them back over. Often times this is timed. With this game, it forces you to work on your short term memory as you try to recall the placement of different images and symbols you just saw a few moments ago.

Rubix Cube

This might be the ultimate memory puzzle game, and also a game individuals boast about beating. Completing a rubix cube is difficult, and challenging, as it forces you to use logic in a three dimensional plane, in order to prove successful. If you can't, than you won't be able to complete it.

Simon Says

There are games where "Simon" tells you to perform several tasks in a row. It starts off with one task, and then it builds up from there. This is going to test your short term memory and determine how long you can go, all without messing up. There are some games there use this practice and utilize lights, sounds and colors, to see if you are able to remember this. It can be difficult, challenging and fun, all at the same time, in order to see if you can follow through with it.

Trivial Pursuit

This is just a fun game that is going to test your knowledge of current affairs, movies, sports and any other trivia you might not know. This is an excellent game to play with friends, and while you might think of it as a memory puzzle, it is forcing you to use areas of your memory you probably haven't in a long time. You might have learned these questions back in high school or in passing, and the game forces you to try and recall the game answers, in order to ensure you are able to complete the task and answer the question.

Chapter 13- Brain Teaser Puzzles

The mind is singularly the most important part of any person. It is an organ that controls every other function of the body. Without it, individuals would cease to function and would be unable to complete even the simplest of tasks. The strength of any muscle, tissue, or organ in our body is determined by the amount of time we dedicate to using that part. For example, the more we use our arms to lift objects, the stronger they become.

The mind is no exception to this idea. That is why it is important for people to continually challenge their brain through daily practice of "neurobotics," a phrase coined by the late Lawrence Katz, a neurologist whose works are associated with the Duke University Medical Center. Different neurobotic activities would include: reading, brainteasers, puzzles, yoga, meditation, and much more.

What Lawrence Katz found is that if one was to use the non-dominant hand to perform simple, daily tasks, is that they could strengthen pathways to the side of the brain that was correlated with their weaker hand. This proves that people are not constrained to the limitations or barriers that their mind may place upon a less dominate section. This proves that people are able to improve upon the functionality of certain areas of the brain if they are to exercise these parts on a more frequent basis. Furthermore, Katz believed that if one were to engage in puzzles, brainteasers, and even just let their mind wander on occasion, they would access certain parts of the brain that are not regularly used. Strengthening these parts of the brain is essential for individuals to function more sharply and even prevent or negate the negative side effects that aging and stress play upon our minds.

Throughout our lives, we are continually generating new brain cells. These new brain cells help our brain function.

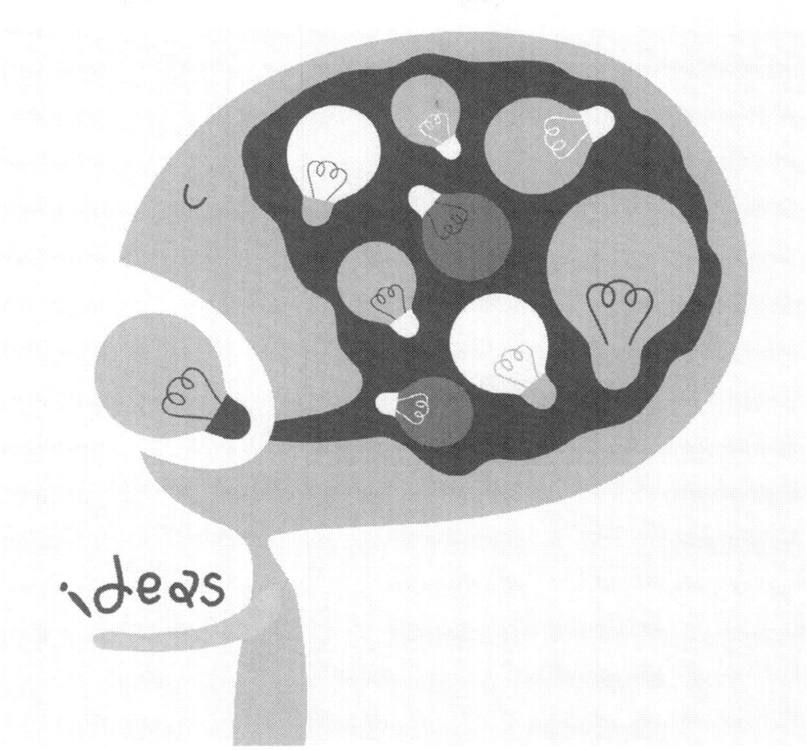

In order to be successful, these new cells must be able to communicate well with each other. In order to do this, the brain cells require that some form of connection be made between them. Brainteasers and other forms of mental exercise have been correlated to the construction of firmly established neural connections between brain cells. An emerging "mini-industry" of brainteasers, puzzles, computer games, etc. has been steadily rising since the beginning of the 21st century. This helps to reinforce the idea that brainteasers and puzzles are effective means of exercising the brain.

Our brain is used to process and execute our will, and we can improve our ability to do this by exercising our brain and making it stronger. Exposing the brain to different brainteasers is small, easy way to exercise the brain, and is not as time consuming as other mental exercises. It is like taking the brain for a light jog, or bringing it to the gym to lift weights. If one is to exercise their brain on a daily basis, they will be able to strengthen their ability to think cognitively.

Old age isn't the only factor that may inhibit the functionality of the brain. Factors such as stress, lack of sleep, and hunger have been proven to be factors that can greatly reduce one's thought process. Many of these factors can be lessened if one makes adjustments to their diet and sleep patterns, but stress is a factor that we generally cannot control. Stress can be brought upon by factors such as workload that a boss places onto individuals, family troubles, and much more. It is important for individuals to maintain a healthy mental exercise habit so they can reduce the "dulling" effect that stress may have on their mind.

This is why the industry of brainteasers and puzzles has evolved into a "mini-industry." Many newspapers and popular magazines have put a small puzzle segment near the end of their publication. Making this segment small is a means of preventing the puzzle or brainteaser from being too daunting of a task for the individual. Consumers may complete these puzzles on their own time, and work on them throughout the day or during a break. These small segments can be a perfect means to escape the daily grind, while also improving upon one's brainpower and preventing the negative effects of aging and stress.

I have included several of my personal favorites brainteasers gathered across the web. Hopefully, they provide the reader with a better understanding of how effective brainteasers can be at exercising the mind. I have also provided the answers to these brainteasers; however, my recommendation to the reader is that they do not look at the answer to the brainteaser until after they have given the teaser ample thought. The reason behind this is that the point of these brainteasers is to exercise the mind. This cannot be done if the reader does not challenge himself or herself.

A man stands on one side of a river, with his dog on the other bank. The man calls for his dog. Without hesitation, the dog crosses the river without using a bridge or boat. The dog does not get wet in the process. How is this possible?

A sundial has the fewest moving parts of any timepiece, which has the most?

Ben's mother had three children. The first child was named April, the second child was named May. What was the third child's name?

Which is correct: "The yolk of the egg is white" or "The yolk of the egg are white?"

If I drink, I die, If I eat, I'm fine. What am I?

What word becomes shorter when you add two letters to it?

What occurs once in a minute, twice in a moment, but never in a thousand years?

I'm tall when I'm young, but short when I'm old. What am I?

Two men play five complete games of chess. Each many wins the same number of games. There are no ties. How is this possible?

A boy was rushed into the hospital's emergency room. The ER doctor took one look at the boy and said, "I cannot operate on this boy, because he is my son." However, the doctor was not the boy's father. How is this possible?

1) The river is frozen

2) An hour glass, with thousands of tiny grains of sand

3) Ben, the answer is given away with the beginning word of the riddle.

4) Neither, egg yolk is yellow.

5) A Fire

6) "Shorter"

7) The letter "M"

8) A candle.

9) The two men were not playing against each other

10) The Doctor was the boy's mother.

CHAPTER 14- DEVELOPING YOUR COGNITIVE SKILLS

Thousands of scientifically researched articles have been written by highly educated people fascinated by how the brain functions. The single organ responsible for building civilization, for raising humanity out of the muck and dirt, the human brain is an extraordinary organic computer that no billion-dollar supercomputer can ever hope to match.

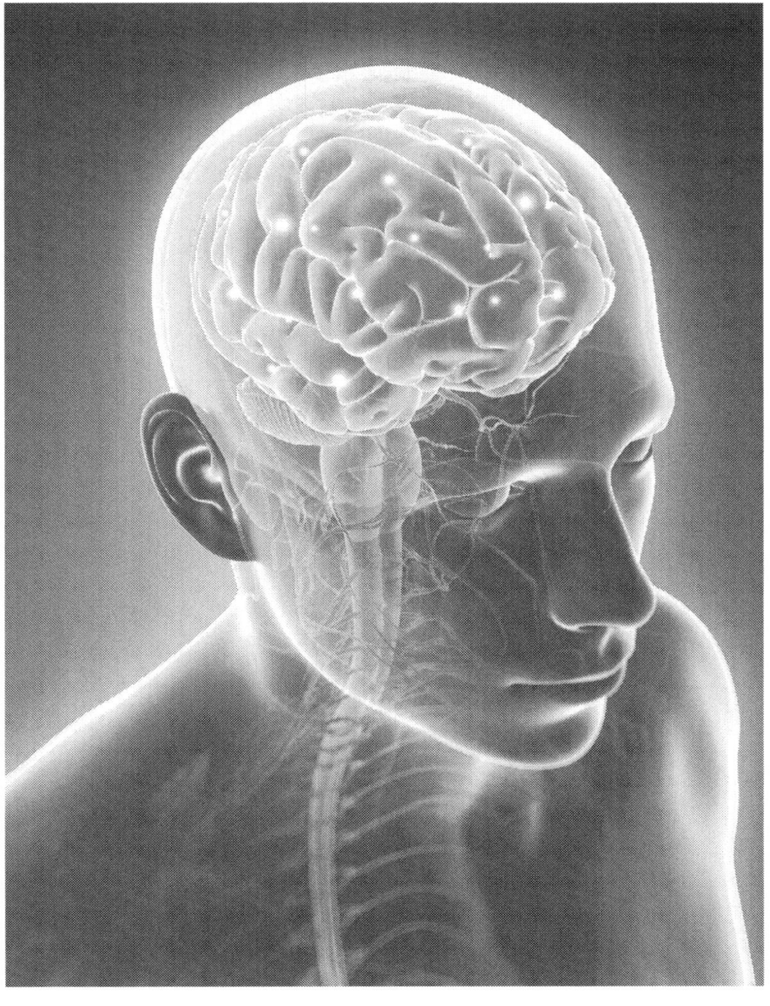

Look at a three-dimensional representation of the brain and we see an electrical storm of activity that looks similar to mock-ups of the universe itself. These layers of complexity are built on the synapses and neurons eternally sparking to transmit thoughts and control autonomic systems of the body. A thought can lead to a voluntary movement, an intake of breath, or the discovery of a new element in the periodic table.

While the fundamental operation of the human brain is mostly known, there are still mysteries, areas of the brain that defy description. Psychologists and neurologists spend decades mapping out the facilities of the brain, seeking the point where thoughts are born, the area of the brain where the mind resides. The comparison of the brain to the universe begins to feel apt, especially considering the amount of exploration remaining.

The fact is, the human brain may never be fully understood, but we know enough to help train the brain, to teach it to eliminate distractions and focus on a single task. Such training can lead to many enhanced facilities, including speed-reading, increased retention of knowledge and greater memory access. Both short-term and long-term memory can benefit from brain training, allowing us to leap forward, magnifying analytic and logical abilities, cognitively boosting performance.

Beginning Brain Training

There's no need to accept the human brain as it is. Imagine instead a muscle that performs only so well in a young athlete because it's untrained. Work out that muscle day after day and its strength is increased and endurance is heightened. The brain is similar, responding to mental workouts and developing in turn.

Lack of activity means fewer connections form, with less synaptic activity, but mental exercises, specially designed by scientific methodology, create greater connectivity within the brain, speeding thoughts and raising mental acuity. Beginner chess players used to observe how their performance in the game improved exponentially as they played more, but they also noticed that a few weeks without playing chess resulted in poor play, more mistakes and a greater amount of lost games.

To continue to perform well, the brain has to be fed a constant stream of oxygen-rich blood and nutrients, but, almost as important as oxygen, the human brain must be exercised and worked with logic and memory strengthening exercises. Memory isn't necessarily an indication of a strong, cognitively able brain. For instance, there are masters of memory who exhibit skills to retain encyclopedic volumes of knowledge, but they're certainly not as smart as an Einstein or Stephen Hawking. Memory is simply one element in the truly cognitive mind. High functioning cognitive thinking involves processing the knowledge, linking it to other concepts and ideas to form new thoughts, creating an awareness of new possibilities and solutions. This is cognitive thought at its most basic but also its best, solving problems and making advanced decisions in fractions of a second based on one or many initial factors. These are the skills that create leaders and presidents, surgeons and scientists.

How to Develop Cognitive Skills

The greatest skill of the brain is its plasticity, its ability to adapt and change when new inputs are applied from our senses. Mathematical puzzles stretch the logical parts of the brain, while drawing and painting, as well as geometric puzzles, activate parts of the brain that deal in both processing logic and spatial awareness. There are many games and skills to accelerate the growth of brain training, with one example being the old Rubik's Cube made popular back in the 1980's. This three-dimensional puzzle exercised the brain in powerful ways, across several dimensions. Speed solvers even used advanced motor skills to solve the puzzle in competitive times.

Neuroplasticity is a science under deep investigation by several branches of science. On one hand, applying puzzles and memory tests works to increase cognitive abilities, but the brain has also amazed us by completely rewiring areas to take over functions that have become damaged. Stroke victims lose the use of speech and the ability to move limbs, but, with practice and hard work, they can recover most of this lost ability. This is a function of the brain that can stop medical experts in their tracks with fascination and wonder.

Cognitive ability is related to the total comprehension of a task and all of its implications, recruiting memory and solution skills to process data. This may sound like a computer but the faculties involved are more complex the interplay more subtle. We have the ability to act and react, to decide or deny and to create entirely new actions, something a computer simply can't do.

A student of brain training must always focus on a task with every fiber of their being, letting the brain process and finesse its decision-making skills until complete comprehension has been achieved. A puzzle or obstacle that at first seemed so complex and impossible becomes easier to master. The amount of steps between the start and completion of a problem become less and less, the brain making new connections to accomplish an exercise in a fraction of the time it first took.

Advanced Cognitive Skills

The potential to accomplish anything is possible with work and focus. Speed-reading comes with heightened comprehension. Memory retention comes with constant training, expanding the brains near limitless capacity. In some ways the poets are right, imagination is our only limit. Visualize being able to memorize complex number sequences, calculate equations completely in our heads and the brain will endeavor to make the skill a reality, sending finely tuned electrical impulses through new bundles of synapse connections. No drugs are required, no special electronic tools, just the dedication and focus to reach beyond what we believe we're capable of.

CROSSWORD PUZZLES

CROSSWORD #1

1	2	3	4	■	5	6	7	8	■	■	■	9	10	11
12				■	13				14	■	15			
16				■	17					■	18			
19				20			■	21		22				
■	■	■	23				■	■	24			■	■	■
25	26	27				■	28	29				30	31	32
33					■	34				■	35			
36			■	■	37					■	■	38		
39			40	■	41				■	42	43			
44				45				■	46					
■	■	■	47			■	■	48				■	■	■
49	50	51				52	■	53				54	55	56
57				■	58		59			■	60			
61				■	62					■	63			
64			■	■	■	65				■	66			

<ACROSS>

1- Heels
5- Sunday seats
9- Capture
12- Came down to earth
13- Marner's creator
15- Slugger Sammy
16- Cancun coin
17- Cost
18- Tied
19- Back part of the skull
21- Having long, narrow grooves
23- Beer buy
24- Kind of reaction
25- Feminine
28- Republic in E Africa
33- Author Calvino
34- Barbarous person
35- Infrequent
36- Flyers' org.
37- ___ the side of caution
38- ___ Tafari (Haile Selassie)
39- Facts and figures
41- Ticked (off)
42- ___ evil...
44- Photograph
46- Idle talk
47- ___ polloi
48- Shank
49- No longer in existence
53- Capital of Armenia
57- In the center of
58- Betel palm
60- Actress Talbot
61- Tins
62- Takes it easy
63- Corp. bigwigs
64- DDE's predecessor
65- Peter Fonda title role
66- Humorist Bombeck

<DOWN>

1- Crime boss
2- One of the Baldwins
3- It may be compact
4- Impassive
5- Read with care
6- Overjoy
7- Finish first
8- Drunkards
9- Bright star
10- I'd hate to break up ___
11- Cause of ruin
14- Make tough
15- Zone
20- ___ Alto
22- Him, to Henri
25- Discovers
26- Patriot Allen
27- Island near Sicily
28- Heron, usually white
29- Walked
30- Trims
31- Teheran native
32- Author of fables
34- Nabisco cookie
37- In the right
40- Plant pests
42- Tart
43- Spirit
45- Male child
46- Lubricant
48- Recurring series
49- "From ___ according to his abilities..."
50- December day, briefly
51- Hue
52- Drop ___ (moon)
54- Contender
55- Mighty mite
56- Rocket launcher
59- Building annex

CROSSWORD #2

1	2	3	4	5	■	6	7	8	■	9	10	11	12	13
14					■	15			■	16				
17					18				■	19				
20			■	■	21				■	22				
■	■	■	23	24			■	■	25					■
26	27	28				■	29	30			■	■	■	■
31						■	32				33	34	35	■
36				■	■	37			■	■	38			39
■	40			41	42			■	43	44				
■	■	■	■	45				■	46					
■	47	48	49			■	■	50				■	■	■
51					■	52	53			■	■	54	55	56
57					■	58				59	60			
61					■	62			■	63				
64					■	65			■	66				

<ACROSS>

1- Roofing stone
6- ___ Tafari (Haile Selassie)
9- Indian state
14- Bit of wisdom
15- Thunder Bay's prov.
16- Twice, a comforting comment
17- Restore moisture
19- Hard drinker
20- Decade divs.
21- Algerian seaport
22- Get the lead out?
23- Old Testament book
25- Refine
26- Aromatic ointment
29- Quick sharp bark
31- Bureau
32- Blue books?
36- Actor Auberjonois
37- Solo of "Star Wars"
38- Iditarod terminus
40- Slowpoke
43- Recorded
45- Crew needs
46- Taoism founder
47- Loud sound
50- Exploded
51- Predatory fish
52- Mata ___
54- Cock and bull
57- Twilled fabric
58- Turn toward the east
61- Place for "stompin'"
62- Hurried
63- Chicago hub
64- Bridges
65- Actor Vigoda
66- Snooped (around)

<DOWN>

1- Agile
2- Lustful look
3- Contented sighs
4- Attempt, a score in rugby
5- Antiquity, in antiquity
6- Lion sounds
7- Organization to promote theater
8- Type of gun
9- Try
10- Beach locale
11- Flower part
12- Give it ___!
13- A ___ formality
18- Spacious
23- Good ___
24- Brit's raincoat
25- ___-pitch softball
26- Ingot
27- Old
28- Actress Olin
29- A long time
30- East ender?
33- Following
34- Paint layer
35- Concert gear
37- That woman
39- Extra-wide shoe size
41- Asses
42- Fall behind
43- Stan's pal
44- Not for a Scot
47- Inexpensive
48- Insect stage
49- Vacuum tube filler
50- Pickling solution
51- Flat sound
52- Circle dance
53- Member of a largely Middle Eastern people
54- Lukas of "Witness"
55- French 101 verb
56- Highly ranked competitor in sporting events
59- Prefix with profit or fiction
60- Howe'er

CROSSWORD #3

1	2	3	4	5	■	6	7	8	9	■	■	10	11	12
13					■	14				■	15			
16					■	17				■	18			
19				■	20					21		■	■	■
■	22			23			■	■	24			25	26	27
■	■	■	28				29	30	■	31				
■	32	33				■	34		35	■	36			
37			■	38		39				40	■	41		
42			43	■	44			■	45		46			■
47				48	■	49		50				■	■	■
51					52	■	■	53				54	55	■
■	■	■	56			57	58			■	59			60
61	62	63		■	64				■	65				
66				■	67				■	68				
69			■	■	70				■	71				

<ACROSS>

1- Experiment
6- Actor Ian
10- Far out!
13- Main artery
14- Inter ___
15- Father
16- Author Dahl
17- Pealed
18- ___ Camera
19- Nick and Nora's pooch
20- The month of May
22- SAT giver
24- Worldly
28- Diners
31- Formula of belief
32- Moisten while cooking
34- A mouse!
36- Antiquing agent
37- A Bobbsey twin
38- Somehow
41- Lilly of pharmaceuticals
42- Miners' sch.
44- Free
45- Actor Christopher
47- Recipient
49- Donny or Marie
51- Snare
53- Help
56- Wave riders
59- Permanent army post
61- Monetary unit of France
64- Word of woe
65- Fungal infection
66- Type of gun
67- 9th letter of the Hebrew alphabet
68- Body of salt water
69- DC bigwig
70- Not difficult
71- Quizzes, trials

<DOWN>

1- Skater Lipinski
2- Perch
3- Steamed
4- Books of maps
5- Boy
6- Capital of Zimbabwe
7- Oil of ___
8- Bits of thread
9- Sleight of hand
10- Narrow inlet
11- Human limb
12- Narc's employer
15- Mountain range
20- Shooting star
21- Brit's raincoat
23- Makes lace
25- Israeli desert region
26- Designer Simpson
27- Actress Petty
29- Orchestra section
30- Attach a patch
32- Wand
33- Concerning
35- South African animal rug
37- Unclothed
39- O Sole ___
40- Longings
43- Individual
46- Building
48- It's bottled in Cannes
50- Soggy and reedy
52- Babble
54- Loudness units
55- Pay for
57- Bloodsucking insect
58- Breaks bread
60- Makes brown
61- Double curve
62- Shoshone language member
63- Cartoon dog
65- Small child

CROSSWORD #4

1	2	3	■	4	5	6	7	■	8	9	10	11	12	13
14			■	15				■	16					
17			■	18				■	19					
20			21					22				■	■	■
23				■	24					■	■	25	26	27
28				29		■	■	30		31	32			
■	■	■	■	33		34	35							
36	37	38	39		■	40			■	41				
42					43				44		■	■	■	■
45							■	■	46		47	48	49	50
51			■	■	52		53	54		■	55			
■	■	■	56	57						58				
59	60	61				■	62				■	63		
64						■	65				■	66		
67						■	68				■	69		

<ACROSS>

1- Takes too much
4- Intend
8- Allege
14- Vietnamese New Year
15- He sang about Alice
16- Planks
17- The 19th letter of the Greek alphabet
18- River sediment
19- One who enjoys inflicting pain
20- Loving
23- Woven fabric
24- Pertaining to the kidneys
25- Numbered rd.
28- Whatever person
30- The act of twisting
33- Hodgepodge
36- Butler's love
40- Feeling of self-importance
41- "Lovergirl" singer ___ Marie
42- Means of supporting life
45- Make sure
46- Valuate
51- Summer drink
52- Fluff, as bangs
55- Ditto
56- Characteristic of journalism
59- Spot on the skin
62- Inter ___
63- Hot time in Paris
64- Accept as true
65- The wolf ___ the door
66- Skin color of Washington football players!
67- Wager
68- Alley
69- Wind dir.

<DOWN>

1- Capital of Canada
2- Destroy hearing
3- Poorly ventilated
4- Not fem.
5- Asmara is its capital
6- Kate & ___
7- ___ your life!
8- Third son of David
9- Layer of paint
10- Mediterranean juniper
11- Altdorf's canton
12- Radical '60s org.
13- Superlative suffix
21- DDE's command
22- Country
25- Teeming
26- Ripped
27- "Only Time" singer
29- Marsh of mystery
31- Gives a 9.8, say
32- Litigate against
34- Mailed communique
35- Bigger than med.
36- Greek peak
37- Colored
38- Busy as ___
39- Queue after Q
43- Locate
44- Southeasternmost hill of Rome
47- Draft org.
48- Diners
49- Strikes
50- Pull out
53- For want of ___...
54- Chip dip
56- Martial art
57- Actor Ken
58- Must've been something ___
59- AT&T rival
60- Upper limb
61- Large, brown-capped mushroom

CROSSWORD #5

1	2	3	4	■	5	6	7	8	■	9	10	11	12	13
14				■	15				■	16				
17				■	18				■	19				
20				■	21				22					
23				■	24			■	25			■	■	■
■	■	■	26	27				28		■	29	30	31	32
33	34	35				■	36			■	37			
38					■	39			■	40				
41				■	42			■	43					
44				■	45			46				■	■	■
■	■	■	47	48		■	49			■	50	51	52	53
54	55	56				57				■	58			
59					■	60				■	61			
62					■	63				■	64			
65					■	66				■	67			

<ACROSS>

1- Shower
5- Pole
9- Pool stroke
14- Corm of the taro
15- Cote d'__
16- Kind of alcohol
17- Mine entrance
18- Bishop of Rome
19- Muse
20- Agricultural implement
21- Something preferred
23- Big rig
24- Comparative suffix
25- Neither's partner
26- Tenseness
29- Melville novel
33- Edible clam
36- PBS benefactor
37- Juniors, perhaps
38- Spring up
39- Mom-and-pop org.
40- Land measures
41- Move suddenly
42- Keats work
43- Lively Spanish dance
44- "Casablanca" role
45- Flapjack
47- Compass dir.
49- Rockers Steely __
50- Pealed
54- Mountain chain
58- Bassoon relative
59- At full speed
60- Bartlett's abbr.
61- Back talk
62- Intervening, in law
63- Home of the Bruins
64- Rapper born Tracy Marrow
65- Catches
66- Stains
67- Team

<DOWN>

1- Harvests
2- Discombobulate
3- Dialect
4- In spite of
5- The act of making maps
6- Islands in the N Atlantic
7- School VIP position
8- Not kosher
9- Paris subway
10- Arterial plaque deposit
11- Type of guard
12- Harmony
13- Actress Sommer
22- "Orinoco Flow" singer
27- Fair-hiring abbr.
28- Some like it hot
30- Oliver Twist's request
31- Doozy
32- __ buco (veal dish)
33- Muslim judge
34- Russian range
35- Broadcasts
39- Palm Pilot, e.g.
40- Hunky-dory
42- German auto
43- Wildly enthusiastic
46- King of pop
48- Dressed to the __
51- Primitive calculators
52- Snooped (around)
53- Beau __
54- Engine parts
55- Predictive sign
56- Tabula __
57- Extol

CROSSWORD #6

1	2	3	4	■	5	6	7	8	■	■	9	10	11	12
13				■	14				15	■	16			
17				■	18					■	19			
■	■	■	20	21				■	22	23				
24	25	26					■	27				■	■	■
28						■	29					30	31	32
33					■	34				■	35			
36			■	■	37					■	■	38		
39			40	■	41				■	42	43			
44				45				■	46					
■	■	■	47				■	48				■	■	■
49	50	51				■	52			■	53	54	55	56
57				■	58	59				■	60			
61				■	62					■	63			
64				■	■	65				■	66			

<ACROSS>	44- Deacidify	21- The world's longest river

<ACROSS>

1- Separate by a sieve
5- ___ Three Lives
9- Periods
13- Comics canine
14- Japanese-American
16- Bern's river
17- American football measure
18- Fills to the gills
19- Religious practice
20- Silly
22- Wheel
24- Continuing
27- Gambling game
28- Separable component
29- African antelope
33- Clear the boards
34- Female child
35- Hydroxyl compound
36- LBJ's successor
37- A Judd
38- Song syllable
39- Assignment
41- Quattro maker
42- Old French expression meaning "goodbye"
44- Deacidify
46- Not us
47- Plunge head-first
48- Chicken cordon ___
49- Bicycle seat
52- Night spot
53- Vex
57- Et ___
58- Synagogue scroll
60- Baseball stats
61- Fail to hit
62- Actress Verdugo
63- Alpo alternative
64- Apiece
65- Bunches
66- Sea-going eagle

<DOWN>

1- Non-dairy milk
2- Highest mountain in Crete
3- Christmas tree
4- Tiresome
5- Certifiable
6- Either of two Chinese dynasties
7- Ferrara family
8- Actress Ruby
9- Ring locale
10- Racetrack boundary
11- Commedia dell'___
12- Prophet
15- Sharon, e.g.
21- The world's longest river
23- Old California fort
24- Code of silence
25- Usual
26- Polish seaport
27- Physicist Enrico
29- ___ Janeiro
30- Free laces, say
31- Kitchen gadget
32- Actor Kinski
34- Surgical dressing
37- Artlessness
40- Liturgical prayer
42- Munched on
43- Nonpile cotton rug of India
45- Dogpatch adjective
46- Dated
48- Game of chance
49- Ditto
50- Inter ___
51- It may be compact
52- Songwriter Jacques
54- Support beam
55- Describe
56- "___ quam videri" (North Carolina's motto)
59- Pay stub?

CROSSWORD #7

1	2	3	4	5	■	6	7	8	9	■	10	11	12	13
14					■	15				■	16			
17					■	18				■	19			
20					21			■	22	23				
■	■	■	24				■	25						
26	27	28				■	29				■	■	■	■
30				■	31	32					33	34	35	36
37				38	■	39			■	40				
41					42				43	■	44			
■	■	■	■	45				■	46	47				
48	49	50	51				■	52				■	■	■
53						■	54					55	56	57
58				■	59	60			■	61				
62				■	63				■	64				
65				■	66				■	67				

<ACROSS>

1- Pundit
6- James of "The Godfather"
10- Deficiency
14- Pie nut
15- Hungary's Nagy
16- Astronaut Shepard
17- Merits
18- Puerto ___
19- Starchy staple
20- Animal
22- Emissary
24- South American monkey
25- Karyokinesis
26- Marked down
29- It's drawn in a lavatory
30- Stadium din
31- Buyers
37- "Who's there?" response
39- ___ favor
40- Low point
41- Service station
44- Big bash
45- Mil. truant
46- Rings bells
48- Dampen
52- Hold on!
53- Except if
54- Breaks
58- "Star Wars" princess
59- Arch type
61- Men
62- Bibliography abbr.
63- Doll's word
64- Dined at home
65- Lays down the lawn
66- Blue-pencil
67- Food and water

<DOWN>

1- Blueprint detail
2- Don
3- Farm unit
4- Soldier
5- Infuse
6- Wispy clouds
7- French friend
8- Rainbow shape
9- Stone relic
10- Key ___
11- AKA
12- Desert bloomers
13- Leg joints
21- Miners' sch.
23- Actor Hawke
25- PC shortcut
26- Not a dup.
27- ___ chance!
28- Disrespectful back talk
29- Oven option
32- Writer Sinclair
33- Shaped like an arrowhead
34- Yellow cheese coated with red wax
35- Irritate
36- Ladies of Sp.
38- Les ___-Unis
42- Inspiring awe
43- Final Four org.
47- Hired killer
48- Some hybrids
49- ___ a customer
50- Greek epic poem
51- Closes
52- Cereal grain
54- Big rig
55- Gen. Robert ___
56- Nevada senator Harry
57- IRS IDs
60- Move about recklessly

CROSSWORD #8

1	2	3	4	■	5	6	7	8	9	■	10	11	12	13
14				■	15					■	16			
17				■	18					19				
20				21	■	22			■	23				
■	■	■	24		25			■	26			■	■	■
27	28	29					■	30				31	32	33
34						■	35				■	36		
37				■	38	39				■	40			
41			■	42				■	43	44				
45			46				■	47						
■	■	■	48			■	49					■	■	■
50	51	52			■	53			■	54		55	56	57
58					59				60	■	61			
62				■	63					■	64			
65				■	66					■	67			

<ACROSS>

1- Just __!
5- Tropical fruit
10- Fire
14- Hindu hero
15- Beaming
16- "A Death in the Family" author
17- Gyro meat
18- Next largest scoop after tea
20- Toothbrush brand
22- Can be used to catch fish or surf!
23- Lacks
24- Wear down, physically or emotionally
26- Use, consume
27- Eyelash cosmetic
30- All together
34- Spanish fleet
35- Queue after Q
36- Imperial unit of weight
37- Neet rival
38- Come into contact with
40- Spanish muralist
41- Part of RSVP
42- Regal address
43- Small sword
45- Voter
47- Stonework
48- Hurried
49- More wan
50- Bee stuff
53- Prince Valiant's son
54- Brother of Moses
58- Treasonable
61- Lady of Spain
62- Driving aids
63- Native Israeli
64- The jig __!
65- Go (over) carefully
66- Precipitous
67- What you do to a joint, prior to a heist

<DOWN>

1- Woody's boy
2- River to the Moselle
3- Austen novel
4- Tramway vehicle
5- Gangster's gun
6- Where Idi Amin ruled
7- "The Zoo Story" playwright
8- Electrical unit
9- Wonder
10- Mexican revolutionist
11- Freudian topics
12- Long time
13- Gave temporarily, holy period of 40 days
19- SeaWorld attraction
21- Actor Pitt
25- Speech
26- Spellbind
27- Parsonage
28- Thin as __
29- Look happy
30- Computer key
31- Beer mug
32- More tender
33- Diary bit
35- Feel bad about
39- Bruins legend
40- Occasional
42- Remains
44- On the briny
46- Wrinkle
47- Excrement used as fertilizer
49- Investigation
50- URL starter
51- Nabisco cookie
52- Not e'en once
53- Med school subj.
55- Parks on a bus
56- Blame
57- Neck part
59- CIA forerunner
60- Drain

CROSSWORD #9

1	2	3	4	■	5	6	7	8	9	■	10	11	12	13
14				■	15					■	16			
17				■	18					■	19			
20				21						22			■	■
■	■	■	■	23			■	■	24			■	■	■
■	25	26	27				28	29				30	31	32
33					■	■	34				■	35		
36				■	37	38				■	39			
40			■	41				■	■	42				
43			44					45	46					■
■	■	■	47			■	■	48			■	■	■	■
■	■	49				50	51				52	53	54	55
56	57			■	58					■	59			
60				■	61					■	62			
63				■	64					■	65			

<ACROSS>

1- Medicinal amount
5- Former French currency
10- Throw
14- Thames town
15- Artist's support
16- Buck follower
17- ___ extra cost
18- Minneapolis suburb
19- Places to sleep
20- Containing fossils
23- The fifth sign of the zodiac
24- Sick
25- Comprehensible
33- Hair net
34- "Hard ___!" (sailor's yell)
35- ___ Lobos
36- Structure for storing grain
37- Ready to hit
39- Civil disturbance
40- RR stop
41- Currency unit of France and Germany, among others
42- 1980 Dom DeLuise film
43- Make lurid
47- Barcelona bear
48- Vane dir.
49- Treat by psychoanalysis
56- 100 centavos
58- ___-car
59- Bring forth young
60- Canadian gas brand
61- Staggering
62- Tirade
63- Env. notation
64- Eye drops
65- Son of Zeus in Greek mythology

<DOWN>

1- Unhearing
2- Director Preminger
3- Juniors, perhaps
4- Slaughter of baseball
5- Tentacle
6- Wirelesses
7- "Clueless" catchphrase
8- Hawaiian goose
9- Woodwind instrument
10- ___ rasa
11- Mine finds
12- Lay down the lawn
13- Distress call
21- ___ Three Lives
22- Shoppe sign word
25- Join forces
26- Atari founder Bushnell
27- Scooby-___
28- Off-limits
29- ___ carte
30- Vigorous attack
31- Unfettered
32- This, in Tijuana
33- Flat sound
37- Absolute ruler
38- Part of TNT
39- Thor Heyerdahl craft
41- New Orleans is The Big ___
42- Bloodsucking insect
44- Already?
45- Less cluttered
46- Historical records
49- Hey, you!
50- Roll call call
51- Draft classification
52- Vega's constellation
53- 365 days
54- Writer Grey
55- Tolkien tree creatures
56- Seed of a legume
57- Cornerstone abbr.

CROSSWORD #10

1	2	3	4	5	■	6	7	8	9	10	■	11	12	13
14					■	15					■	16		
17					■	18					■	19		
■	■	■	■	20	21				■	22	23			
24	25	26	27				■	■	28					
29						■	30	31				■	■	■
32				■	33	34				■	35	36	37	38
39				■	■	40			■	■	41			
42				■	43				44	■	45			
■	■	■	46	47				■	48	49				
50	51	52				■	■	53						
54					■	55	56				■	■	■	■
57			■	58	59				■	60	61	62	63	64
65			■	66					■	67				
68			■	69					■	70				

<ACROSS>

1- Novelist Joyce Carol ___
6- A Musketeer
11- Georgia, once: Abbr.
14- Value
15- Song of joy
16- Scot's refusal
17- Nobelist Root
18- Japanese porcelain
19- "Wheel of Fortune" buy
20- Male voice
22- Like some infections
24- Brother or sister
28- Trojan War hero
29- New settlement
30- Assembly rooms
32- Getting ___ years
33- Alert
35- Soviet news agency
39- Circular band
40- Sugary suffix
41- ___ breve
42- Babe in the woods
43- ___ luck!
45- Tenn. Neighbor
46- Dwelling
48- Puget Sound city
50- Winter vehicle
53- Let loose
54- Actress Sophia
55- Shaft shot from a bow
57- ___ standstill
58- Take ___ at (try)
60- Valuable violin
65- Little one
66- Currency unit in Nigeria
67- Approvals
68- Vane dir.
69- Colorado resort
70- Brown and white Eurasian falcon

<DOWN>

1- Be in the red
2- "You've got mail" co.
3- Part of TNT
4- Biblical verb ending
5- Recluse
6- Imitating
7- ___ -shanter (Scottish cap)
8- Listen to
9- Implement used when rowing a boat
10- Whine
11- Animal trap
12- Capital city of Yemen
13- Staggers
21- "Only Time" singer
23- Example
24- Disdain
25- Ancient region of Asia Minor
26- Russian pancakes
27- Gloomy expression
28- Malt beverage
30- Speed
31- Son of Zeus in Greek mythology
34- Timber
36- Foil maker
37- Bridge feats
38- Mother of Isaac
43- Destiny
44- ___ extra cost
47- Tropical fruit
49- Continuously
50- List of candidates
51- ___ your life!
52- Use a soapbox
53- Living in a city
55- Take ___ from me
56- Infrequent
59- Airline to Oslo
61- Give ___ break!
62- Pop the question
63- Type of shirt
64- Leb. neighbor

CROSSWORD #11

1	2	3	4	■	5	6	7	8	9	■	10	11	12	13
14				■	15					■	16			
17				■	18					■	19			
■	20			21						22				
■	■	■	23					■	■	24				
25	26	27				■	■	28	29			■	■	■
30				■	■	31	32					33	34	35
36			■	37	38						■	39		
40			41					■	■	42				
■	■	■	43				■	■	44	45				
46	47	48			■	■	49	50				■	■	■
51					52	53						54	55	■
56				■	57					■	58			59
60				■	61					■	62			
63				■	64					■	65			

<ACROSS>

1- Go downhill fast?
5- Copper and zinc alloy
10- Cookbook amts.
14- Used to be
15- Cost
16- British nobleman
17- Long fish
18- Duck with soft down
19- Bacchanalian cry
20- Agent
23- Seeps
24- Dogma
25- Within
28- Chemical used on trees
30- London jail
31- 3-point printing type
36- Texas tea
37- Official permit
39- Brandy letters
40- Fluke
42- Gaucho's weapon
43- Object of devotion
44- Intense fear
46- Hosiery thread
49- Mouthlike opening
51- Executive
56- Tidy
57- Anticipate
58- Bean town?
60- Wife of Shiva
61- Twinned crystal
62- Hula hoops?
63- ___ breve
64- Genre
65- Ferrara family

<DOWN>

1- Nor. neighbor
2- Lecherous look
3- Author ___ Stanley Gardner
4- Pillage
5- Current of air
6- Elevate
7- Aconcagua's range
8- Type of gun
9- Category
10- Seesaws
11- Eurasian juniper
12- Establish as the truth
13- Driving hazard
21- Slender bar
22- Start of a Dickens title
25- ___ Rhythm
26- Neet rival
27- Boot bottom
28- Teen spots?
29- Bandleader Brown
31- Earth Day subj.
32- Crossed (out)
33- Actor Novello
34- Capital of Norway
35- Crowd sound
37- Burdened
38- Simpson trial judge
41- Citizen army
42- Blind system of writing
44- Perfectly
45- 911 respondent
46- Sri ___
47- Model
48- Little
49- Actor Keach
50- Run of bird-song
52- Alpo alternative
53- Attack a fly
54- Contends
55- Expel gas or odor
59- Enzyme ending

CROSSWORD #12

1	2	3	4	■	■	■	5	6	7	■	8	9	10	11
12				13	■	14				■	15			
16					■	17				■	18			
19					20			■	21	22				
■	■	■	■	23			■	24			■	25		
26	27	28	29			■	30				31	■	■	■
32					■	33						34	35	36
37				■	38					■	39			
40				41					■	42				
■	■	■	43					■	44					
45	46	47	■	48			■	49			■	■	■	■
50			51			■	52				53	54	55	56
57				■	58	59			■	60				
61				■	62				■	63				
64				■	65			■	■	■	66			

<ACROSS>

1- Scrutinize
5- Fore's partner
8- Trudge
12- Apartment sign
14- Ali ____ & the 40 thieves
15- Carry
16- Muscat native
17- Stumble
18- Very small quantity
19- Type of ballot
21- More strange
23- Freight weight
24- Superlative suffix
25- Hesitant sounds
26- Dealer in textiles
30- Showed interest
32- For all to hear
33- The act of retrieving
37- Split
38- Frothy
39- ___ -shanter (Scottish cap)
40- Observe with festivities
42- Stroll
43- Debris
44- Soundless
45- Yale student
48- Classic two-seaters
49- Grog ingredient
50- Angel of the highest order
52- Remembrance
57- Tailless amphibian
58- Shipping deduction
60- Unit of volume
61- Get in a hand
62- Oklahoma city
63- Name on a bomber
64- Honey producers
65- Figs.
66- CPR experts

<DOWN>

1- Greek portico
2- Hair untangler
3- Word of woe
4- Hawaiian goose
5- River in central Switzerland
6- Law enforcement agency
7- Hand woven pictorial design
8- Agitate
9- Sarge's superior
10- Furry swimmer
11- Toothed wheels
13- Colored
14- Bingo call
20- Craggy hill
22- Sewing case
24- Words on a Wonderland cake
26- Not fem.
27- Fashion mag
28- Stir up
29- More adorable
30- Chairs
31- Flower segment
33- Some horses
34- Urn
35- "So be it"
36- Booty
38- Terrify
41- Collide with
42- Zit
44- Litigate against
45- Cornerstone abbr.
46- Sierra ___
47- Angry
49- Vibrating component of a woodwind instrument
51- Summer coolers
52- Actor Kristofferson
53- Cosecant's reciprocal
54- Smallest component
55- Salmon that has spawned
56- Periods
59- Year abroad

CROSSWORD #13

<ACROSS>

1- Chilean pianist Claudio
6- South American Indian
10- Buddies
14- Bank offerings
15- Tattled
16- Nabisco treat
17- African language group
18- Old oath
19- Actress Anderson
20- Like llamas
22- Novel
24- Grazing spot
26- Inflammation of the ear
27- Having a resemblance
31- ___ du Diable
32- Like tongues of fire
33- Sign up
36- EMT's skill
39- Cop's collar
40- Faint
41- River in central Switzerland
42- HST's successor
43- Scenes
44- Distribute
45- Blink of an eye
46- State of decline
48- Animated
51- Prefix meaning "beneath"
52- Ornamental headband
54- Talks back to
59- On ___ with
60- Actor Morales
62- ___ bleu!
63- Routine
64- Spanish muralist
65- Busy
66- Historic Scott
67- IRS IDs
68- Discourage

<DOWN>

1- Jessica of "Dark Angel"
2- Horse color
3- McNally's partner
4- Get in a hand
5- Normally
6- Mineral suffix
7- Canceled
8- Mild cigar
9- Opposite of subtraction
10- Courteous
11- Rice-___
12- Horne and Olin
13- Dirty
21- PBS benefactor
23- Fish feature
25- ___ there yet?
27- Dirty Harry's org.
28- ___ Three Lives
29- Female horse
30- Mischievous child
34- At the present time
35- Thorny flowers
36- Colombian city
37- Goad
38- Nerve network
40- Illness
41- Cockpit abbr.
43- Aloe ___
44- Caliph from Baghdad
45- Consecrated
47- Student's conveyance
48- Flavor
49- Babble
50- Approvals
52- Ace, e.g.
53- Mountain lake
55- Having a sound mind
56- Rabbit's tail
57- Gaelic language of Ireland or Scotland
58- Clairvoyant
61- T.G.I.F. part

CROSSSWORD #14

1	2	3	4		5	6	7	8	9		10	11	12	13
14					15						16			
17					18						19			
20				21					22	23				
			24					25						
26	27	28						29				30	31	32
33						34	35					36		
37					38							39		
40					41					42	43			
44			45	46					47					
			48						49					
50	51	52					53	54				55	56	57
58					59	60					61			
62					63						64			
65					66						67			

<ACROSS>

1- Bar bills
5- Appliance brand
10- Sea east of the Caspian
14- Killed
15- Tribunal
16- Vessel
17- Go (over) carefully
18- Cuban dance
19- Album unit
20- Miscellaneous items
22- Midday nap
24- Summer Games org.
25- Flat sound
26- Festival
29- Lighter-than-air craft
33- D-Day beach
34- Jazz flutist Herbie
36- Barcelona bear
37- Lion, tiger, leopard, or jaguar
38- Label anew
39- ACLU concerns
40- Turkish title
41- On the briny
42- Boat often made of birchbark, canvas, or fiberglass
44- Correspondences
47- Some sculptures
48- ___-deucey
49- Goal, intention
50- Zone
53- Like a significant moment in time
58- ___ monde
59- That is, in Latin
61- New Rochelle college
62- Nabisco treat
63- Hostess Mesta
64- Mysterious character
65- Prefix with skeleton
66- Relaxed
67- School founded in 1440

<DOWN>

1- Cookbook amts.
2- Baseball family name
3- Capital on the Aare
4- Start for fish, meatballs, or massage
5- Second-largest continent
6- Pout
7- Weaponry
8- Essence
9- Collecting
10- Evaluate
11- Pi followers
12- Isn't wrong?
13- Annika Sorenstam's org.
21- Roster used to assign duties
23- Leb. neighbor
25- Capital city of Yemen
26- ____ point: where it all becomes clear
27- Icon
28- Really bother
30- Hard outgrowths
31- Playground retort
32- Assumed attitudes
34- Unordered
35- Corroded
38- Early fruit
42- San Francisco's ___ Tower
43- Movable cupboard
45- Body art
46- Green prefix
47- Sampled
50- Foot covering
51- Deserve
52- Prompted
53- Towel word
54- Wight or Man
55- Lopsided victory
56- ___ uncertain terms
57- Capital of Calvados, in NW France
60- Narc's employer

CROSSWORD #15

1	2	3	4	5	6	7	8	■	9	10	11	12	13	14
15								■	16					
17								■	18					
19			■	20			■	■	■	21				
22			23	■	24		25	26	27		■	28		
29				30		■	31				■	32		
■	33				■	34					35			■
■	■	■	36		37							■	■	■
■	38	39							■	40		41	42	■
43			■	44				■	45					46
47			■	48				49		■	50			
51			52		■	■	■	53		54	■	55		
56					57	■	58				59			
60						■	61							
62						■	63							

<ACROSS>

1- One who deals in small craft
9- California peak
15- Toothless
16- Putrid
17- Portrayed
18- Having sound
19- Naval rank, briefly
20- ___-disant (self-styled)
21- Law of Moses
22- Film ___
24- Jumpy
28- Compass dir.
29- Bright golden brown
31- Horse color
32- PIN requester
33- Group of two
34- Stabilizes
36- Swelling
38- Interlocution
40- Oscar winner Patricia
43- Russert of "Meet the Press"
44- Nicholas II, for one
45- Grommet
47- Charlottesville sch.
48- Regard
50- Magma
51- Sucrose
53- Calendar abbr.
55- Singer Torme
56- Culmination
58- Somite
60- Related through males
61- Explosive shells
62- Required
63- Not extreme

<DOWN>

1- Didn't exist
2- Tonsil's neighbor
3- Tenseness
4- Conclusion
5- Numbered rds.
6- Dark brownish red color
7- Dined at home
8- Actor Beatty
9- Grads-to-be
10- Informal folk concert
11- ___ extra cost
12- Ogle
13- Lease holders
14- Hymn
23- Gaucho's rope
25- Sign of a slip
26- Soft
27- Strong wind
30- Make impure
34- Sired
35- Alloy of iron and carbon
37- Rock clinging plant
38- Communicate
39- Conceive
41- Oakland's county
42- Young hare
43- From Florence, e.g.
45- Chewed the scenery
46- "Honor Thy Father" author
49- Diciembre follower
52- Diary of ___ Housewife
54- Windmill part
57- Crossed (out)
58- "The Wizard of Oz" studio
59- Blemish

CROSSWORD #16

1	2	3	4	5	■	6	7	8	9	10	■	11	12	13
14					■	15					■	16		
17					■	18					■	19		
■	■	■	■	20	21			■	■	22	23			
24	25	26	27				■	28	29					■
30						■	31					■	■	■
32					■	33						34	35	36
37			■	■	38					■	■	39		
40			41	42					■	43	44			
■	■	■	45					■	46					
■	47	48					■	49						
50					■	■	51				■	■	■	■
52			■	53	54	55			■	56	57	58	59	60
61			■	62					■	63				
64			■	65					■	66				

<ACROSS>

1- George of "Just Shoot Me"
6- Tirades
11- Star Wars letters
14- Gaze intently
15- Fool
16- 1963 Paul Newman film
17- Elevate
18- Raccoon relative
19- Very cold
20- ___ on first?
22- Related to the kidneys
24- Ancient Egyptian king
28- Sharon's land
30- Go back
31- Two cents, so to speak
32- Ventilated
33- Aversion
37- Lilt syllable
38- Actress Barkin
39- Caviar
40- Indispensable
43- Amulet
45- Continue a subscription
46- Starvation
47- Island off the SE coast of China
49- Dampen
50- Female sovereign
51- Horn warning
52- Not to mention
53- Lucy's landlady
56- Busy
61- Actress Ruby
62- Sex researcher Hite
63- More delicate
64- Fingers
65- Oozes
66- Throw with force

<DOWN>

1- Georgia, once: Abbr.
2- LAX posting
3- Moo goo ___ pan
4- Horace's "___ Poetica"
5- Lee side
6- Big name in copiers
7- Brouhahas
8- Actress Peeples
9- Small drink, young child
10- Stapes
11- Glisten
12- Noble, in a way
13- Pastoral poem
21- Darlin'
23- I could ___ horse!
24- Babble
25- They've got something coming
26- Gillette razors
27- Regret
28- Chip maker
29- Whirl
31- Relative by marriage
33- Extraterrestrial
34- Distinguishing characteristic
35- Mezzo-soprano Marilyn
36- Arabian republic
38- Sicilian volcano
41- Buffalo's county
42- Novelty
43- Villain
44- ___ Pinafore
46- Rock's ___ Fighters
47- Adjusted pitch
48- Yellow-fever mosquito
49- Burrowing animals
50- Muslim judge
51- Maryland athlete, for short
54- Common article
55- Tee follower
57- Latin word meaning "nothing"
58- Verse starter?
59- D.C. VIP
60- Unit of energy

CROSSWORD #17

1	2	3	4	5	■	6	7	8	9	10	■	11	12	13
14					■	15					■	16		
17					■	18					19			
20			■	21	22			■	■	23				
■	■	24	25				■	26	27					
28	29					■	30					■	■	■
31					■	32					■	33	34	35
36				■	37					■	38			
39			■	40					■	41				
■	■	■	42					■	43					
44	45	46					■	47					■	■
48					■	■	49				■	50	51	52
53					54	55			■	56	57			
58			■	59					■	60				
61			■	62					■	63				

<ACROSS>

1- Punctuation mark
6- Tire (out)
11- Doctrine
14- Bellowing
15- Skirt style
16- Cry ___ River
17- Country singer Tucker
18- Thin, delicate printing surface
20- ___-pitch softball
21- Big cheese
23- Ogles
24- Cost
26- Surly
28- Financially solvent
30- Bahamanian island
31- Hanker
32- Fit to be tied
33- Scandinavian rug
36- Start of a counting rhyme
37- Takes it easy
38- Mariners can sail on seven of these
39- Compass dir.
40- Monopoly buy
41- Island in the Bay of Naples
42- Horne and Olin
43- Decorative band
44- Money put aside for the future
47- Take the honey and run
48- Dress with care
49- Conductor Klemperer
50- Tropical cuckoo bird
53- Reconciliation
56- Praise
58- Cambodia's Lon ___
59- Jazzy Chick
60- Actress Verdugo
61- Hawaiian acacia
62- Boat spines
63- Jeter of the Yankees

<DOWN>

1- Burmese, Manx, and Scottish Fold
2- Spoken
3- Airplane with one set of wings
4- Spring month
5- High-spirited horse
6- Analyze a sentence
7- Some Ivy Leaguers
8- Personal quirk
9- Wind dir.
10- Provide a substitute for
11- Rock and Roll Hall of Fame architect
12- Prophets
13- Waterlogged soil
19- Dynamic beginning
22- Fall mo.
25- Actor Calhoun
26- Hoops
27- Breaks bread
28- Affirmative votes
29- Professional charges
30- City on the Rhone
32- Tiny amounts
33- A second pleading
34- Dextrous, lively
35- Be that ___ may...
37- Protracted
38- Coarsely ground corn
40- Domineer a husband
41- Not straight
42- Describe
43- Cockpit abbr.
44- Paddle
45- Threepio's buddy
46- Orchestra string
47- Kett and James
49- Like Nash's lama
51- Nada
52- Writer Dinesen
54- "The Simpsons" bartender
55- Before, of yore
57- Suffix with glob

CROSSWORD #18

1	2	3	4	5	6		7	8	9		10	11	12	13
14							15				16			
17							18				19			
			20			21				22				
23	24	25				26				27				
28					29				30					
31				32				33				34	35	36
37				38				39				40		
41				42				43			44			
			45				46				47			
48	49	50				51				52				
53					54				55					
56					57				58			59	60	61
62					63				64					
65					66				67					

<ACROSS>

1- Capital of the Philippines
7- CD-___
10- Baby powder
14- Lets up
15- Altar in the sky
16- "East of Eden" director Kazan
17- Dwarfed tree
18- Droop, sink
19- K-6
20- Loving
23- Inspire anew
26- ___ kwon do
27- Playground retort
28- Yours, in Tours
29- Cambodia's Lon ___
30- Foxy
31- Breed of dog unable to bark
33- Numbered rd.
34- This ___ stickup!
37- Exist
38- "You've got mail" co.
39- Attention
40- Romanian coin
41- ___ the season...
42- Opposite of post-
43- Angling
45- Free
46- Central
47- Leisure
48- First name in cosmetics
51- Proverb ending?
52- Bird that gets you down
53- Vexing
56- Growl
57- Actor Erwin
58- North African desert
62- Farm unit
63- Flub
64- Besides
65- Take it easy
66- Female rabbit
67- Monster's nickname

<DOWN>

1- Fairy queen
2- Blood letters
3- A Bobbsey twin
4- I've been framed!
5- Like spinach
6- "Clueless" catchphrase
7- Mischievous person
8- Use a soapbox
9- Wise trio
10- Wee
11- ___ once
12- Mislead
13- Walk-on role
21- Prima ballerina
22- Edmonton team
23- Capital on the Atlantic
24- Maker of Pong
25- Misplaces
29- Norse god of winds
30- Sedate
32- Inventor of logarithms
33- Ballpoint insert
34- Greek epic poem
35- Have a feeling
36- Boring tool
44- Elevations
45- Sense of loss
46- Ripe
48- Mystery writer's award
49- Subsequently
50- Former Russian rulers
51- Emcee's job
52- Related on the mother's side
54- Second hand, took advantage of
55- This ___ outrage!
59- Sighs of relief
60- Thor Heyerdahl craft
61- Bolted down

CROSSWORD #19

1	2	3	4	5	■	6	7	8	9	■	10	11	12	13
14					■	15				■	16			
17					■	18				■	19			
20					21			■	22	23				
■	■	■	24				■	25						
26	27	28				■	29				■	■	■	■
30				■	31	32					33	34	35	36
37				38	■	39			■	40				
41					42				43	■	44			
■	■	■	■	45				■	46	47				
48	49	50	51				■	52				■	■	■
53						■	54					55	56	57
58				■	59	60			■	61				
62				■	63				■	64				
65				■	66				■	67				

<ACROSS>

1- Capital city of Yemen
6- Petty quarrel
10- Mogul capital until 1658
14- Goes into business
15- Like some excuses
16- Ship's company
17- Eats to a plan
18- That's ___!
19- Ike's ex
20- One after another
22- One making fun
24- Fishing reel
25- Unit of magnetic intensity
26- Wild sheep of Asia
29- Trading center
30- Castle ring
31- Proprietor of a bookstore
37- Zero
39- Capote, to friends
40- You ___ mouthful!
41- Homebody
44- Author Harte
45- Sharp
46- Everett of "Citizen Kane"
48- Explorer
52- Former Russian ruler
53- Gnawing animal
54- First public performance
58- ___ about (approximately)
59- Give an edge to
61- Arbor
62- Feathered creature
63- "East of Eden" director Kazan
64- Songs for two
65- New Orleans is The Big ___
66- Tirade
67- It's a good thing

<DOWN>

1- Lays down the lawn
2- ...baked in ___
3- Not e'en once
4- Aversion
5- Beset
6- Killed
7- Inner surface of the hand
8- Parisian pal
9- Seesaws
10- Take the role of
11- Grain to be ground
12- Actress Taylor
13- Give merit
21- Chicago paper, for short
23- Some Art Deco works
25- Loose fiber used for caulking
26- Latin 101 word
27- Defeat decisively
28- Infatuated
29- Stupid person
32- Alternate
33- Industrious
34- Old Italian money
35- Biblical garden
36- Appraise
38- Captivated (by)
42- Baby's ring
43- "___ quam videri" (North Carolina's motto)
47- Kappa follower
48- Investigation
49- Ancient Greek colony
50- Smells
51- Dweebish
52- Pay for
54- Nabokov novel
55- More than one female sheep
56- Nerve network
57- Formerly, once
60- Pay stub?

CROSSWORD #20

1	2	3	4		5	6	7	8	9		10	11	12	13
14					15						16			
17					18						19			
20				21						22				
			23					24	25					
26	27	28		29			30		31			32	33	34
35			36			37		38			39			
40					41						42			
43					44					45				
46				47			48		49			50		
			51			52		53			54			
55	56	57				58	59					60	61	62
63					64						65			
66					67						68			
69					70						71			

<ACROSS>

1- Shape
5- With cunning
10- Lukas of "Witness"
14- Again
15- Turkish title
16- Ratio phrase
17- Dagger of yore
18- Girder
19- Greek portico
20- Bullfighters
22- Flight of steps
23- Uncle Remus title
24- Horton Hears ___
26- Onetime Jeep mfr.
29- Chicago paper, for short
31- Add fizz
35- Freedom from war
37- Spoken
39- Gotcha
40- As a result
41- Sound of a duck
42- Away from the wind
43- Antiquing agent
44- Bhutan's continent
45- Catches
46- Panel of special keys
48- Mont. neighbor
50- Believer's suffix
51- Cut out
53- Actor Estrada
55- The end of ___
58- Women collectively
63- Pineapple vendor
64- Passover feast
65- ___ Lisa
66- "Puppy Love" singer
67- Mrs. Gorbachev
68- ___'acte (intermission)
69- Film unit
70- Shooting sport
71- Pan's opposite

<DOWN>

1- Sail support
2- ___ account (never)
3- Sly look
4- Nerd
5- Arachnid
6- Industrious
7- River of Flanders
8- Capital of Tibet
9- Sweet potato
10- Chronicler
11- Hammett hound
12- Yours, in Tours
13- Rise sharply, as a bird would
21- Commedia dell'___
22- Female pronoun
25- Travel on foot
26- More or less vertical
27- Unite
28- Cautious
30- Central nervous system
32- Opponent of Ike
33- Supermodel Cheryl
34- Discharge
36- Tangible
38- Pseudo-intellectual speech
41- Muslim judge
45- Pelt
47- Doc bloc
49- Turkey's highest peak
52- Fine-tune
54- Inhabitant of Cambodia
55- Purim month
56- Zero
57- Actress Sommer
59- Comics canine
60- A Chaplin
61- Airing
62- Challenge to complete a task
64- Grads-to-be

Answers

CROSSWORD #1

1 C	2 A	3 D	4 S	■	5 P	6 E	7 W	8 S	■	■	■	9 N	10 A	11 B
12 A	L	I	T	■	13 E	L	I	O	14 T	■	15 S	O	S	A
16 P	E	S	O	■	17 R	A	N	T	O	■	18 E	V	E	N
19 O	C	C	I	20 P	U	T	■	21 S	U	22 L	C	A	T	E
■	■	■	23 C	A	S	E	■	■	24 G	U	T	■	■	■
25 F	26 E	27 M	A	L	E	■	28 E	29 T	H	I	O	30 P	31 I	32 A
33 I	T	A	L	O	■	34 O	G	R	E	■	35 R	A	R	E
36 N	H	L	■	■	37 E	R	R	O	N	■	■	38 R	A	S
39 D	A	T	40 A	■	41 T	E	E	D	■	42 S	43 E	E	N	O
44 S	N	A	P	45 S	H	O	T	■	46 G	O	S	S	I	P
■	■	■	47 H	O	I	■	■	48 C	R	U	S	■	■	■
49 E	50 X	51 T	I	N	C	52 T	■	53 Y	E	R	E	54 V	55 A	56 N
57 A	M	I	D	■	58 A	59 R	E	C	A	■	60 N	I	T	A
61 C	A	N	S	■	62 L	O	L	L	S	■	63 C	E	O	S
64 H	S	T	■	■	■	65 U	L	E	E	■	66 E	R	M	A

CROSSWORD #2

1 S	2 L	3 A	4 T	5 E	■	6 R	7 A	8 S	■	9 A	10 S	11 S	12 A	13 M
14 P	E	A	R	L	■	15 O	N	T	■	16 T	H	E	R	E
17 R	E	H	Y	D	18 R	A	T	E	■	19 T	O	P	E	R
20 Y	R	S	■	■	21 O	R	A	N	■	22 E	R	A	S	E
■	■	■	23 A	24 M	O	S	■	■	25 S	M	E	L	T	■
26 B	27 A	28 L	S	A	M	■	29 Y	30 E	L	P	■	■	■	■
31 A	G	E	N	C	Y	■	32 E	R	O	T	33 I	34 C	35 A	■
36 R	E	N	E	■	■	37 H	A	N	■	■	38 N	O	M	39 E
■	40 D	A	W	41 D	42 L	E	R	■	43 O	44 N	T	A	P	E
■	■	■	■	45 O	A	R	S	■	46 L	A	O	T	S	E
■	47 C	48 L	49 A	N	G	■	■	50 B	L	E	W	■	■	■
51 S	H	A	R	K	■	52 H	53 A	R	I	■	■	54 H	55 E	56 S
57 S	E	R	G	E	■	58 O	R	I	E	59 N	60 T	A	T	E
61 S	A	V	O	Y	■	62 R	A	N	■	63 O	H	A	R	E
64 S	P	A	N	S	■	65 A	B	E	■	66 N	O	S	E	D

CROSSWORD #3

1 T	2 R	3 I	4 A	5 L	■	6 H	7 O	8 L	9 M	■	■	10 R	11 A	12 D
13 A	O	R	T	A	■	14 A	L	I	A	■	15 S	I	R	E
16 R	O	A	L	D	■	17 R	A	N	G	■	18 I	A	M	A
19 A	S	T	A	■	20 M	A	Y	T	I	21 M	E	■	■	■
■	22 T	E	S	23 T	E	R	■	■	24 C	A	R	25 N	26 A	27 L
■	■	■	28 E	A	T	E	29 R	30 S	■	31 C	R	E	D	O
■	32 B	33 A	S	T	E	■	34 E	E	35 K	■	36 A	G	E	R
37 N	A	N	■	38 S	O	39 M	E	W	A	40 Y	■	41 E	L	I
42 U	T	E	43 P	■	44 R	I	D	■	45 R	E	46 E	V	E	■
47 D	O	N	E	48 E	■	49 O	S	50 M	O	N	D	■	■	■
51 E	N	T	R	A	52 P	■	■	53 A	S	S	I	54 S	55 T	■
■	■	■	56 S	U	R	57 F	58 E	R	S	■	59 F	O	R	60 T
61 E	62 U	63 R	O	■	64 A	L	A	S	■	65 T	I	N	E	A
66 S	T	E	N	■	67 T	E	T	H	■	68 O	C	E	A	N
69 S	E	N	■	■	70 E	A	S	Y	■	71 T	E	S	T	S

CROSSWORD #4

1 O	2 D	3 S	■	4 M	5 E	6 A	7 N	■	8 A	9 C	10 C	11 U	12 S	13 E
14 T	E	T	■	15 A	R	L	O	■	16 B	O	A	R	D	S
17 T	A	U	■	18 S	I	L	T	■	19 S	A	D	I	S	T
20 A	F	F	21 E	C	T	I	O	22 N	A	T	E	■	■	■
23 W	E	F	T	■	24 R	E	N	A	L	■	■	25 R	26 T	27 E
28 A	N	Y	O	29 N	E	■	■	30 T	O	31 R	32 S	I	O	N
■	■	■	■	33 G	A	34 L	35 L	I	M	A	U	F	R	Y
36 O	37 H	38 A	39 R	A	■	40 E	G	O	■	41 T	E	E	N	A
42 S	U	B	S	I	43 S	T	E	N	44 C	E	■	■	■	■
45 S	E	E	T	O	I	T	■	■	46 A	S	47 S	48 E	49 S	50 S
51 A	D	E	■	■	52 T	E	53 A	54 S	E	■	55 S	A	M	E
■	■	■	56 J	57 O	U	R	N	A	L	58 I	S	T	I	C
59 M	60 A	61 C	U	L	A	■	62 A	L	I	A	■	63 E	T	E
64 C	R	E	D	I	T	■	65 I	S	A	T	■	66 R	E	D
67 I	M	P	O	N	E	■	68 L	A	N	E	■	69 S	S	E

CROSSWORD #5

1 R	2 A	3 I	4 N	■	5 M	6 A	7 S	8 T	■	9 M	10 A	11 S	12 S	13 E
14 E	D	D	O	■	15 A	Z	U	R	■	16 E	T	H	Y	L
17 A	D	I	T	■	18 P	O	P	E	■	19 T	H	I	N	K
20 P	L	O	W	■	21 P	R	E	F	22 E	R	E	N	C	E
23 S	E	M	I	■	24 I	E	R	■	25 N	O	R	■	■	■
■	■	■	26 T	27 E	N	S	I	28 T	Y	■	29 O	30 M	31 O	32 O
33 Q	34 U	35 A	H	O	G	■	36 N	E	A	■	37 S	O	N	S
38 A	R	I	S	E	■	39 P	T	A	■	40 A	C	R	E	S
41 D	A	R	T	■	42 O	D	E	■	43 B	O	L	E	R	O
44 I	L	S	A	■	45 P	A	N	46 C	A	K	E	■	■	■
■	■	■	47 N	48 N	E	■	49 D	A	N	■	50 R	51 A	52 N	53 G
54 C	55 O	56 R	D	I	L	57 L	E	R	A	■	58 O	B	O	E
59 A	M	A	I	N	■	60 A	N	O	N	■	61 S	A	S	S
62 M	E	S	N	E	■	63 U	C	L	A	■	64 I	C	E	T
65 S	N	A	G	S	■	66 D	Y	E	S	■	67 S	I	D	E

CROSSWORD #6

1 S	2 I	3 F	4 T	■	5 I	6 L	7 E	8 D	■	■	9 E	10 R	11 A	12 S
13 O	D	I	E	■	14 N	I	S	E	15 I	■	16 A	A	R	E
17 Y	A	R	D	■	18 S	A	T	E	S	■	19 R	I	T	E
■	■	■	20 I	21 N	A	N	E	■	22 R	23 O	L	L	E	R
24 O	25 N	26 G	O	I	N	G	■	27 F	A	R	O	■	■	■
28 M	O	D	U	L	E	■	29 R	E	E	D	B	30 U	31 C	32 K
33 E	R	A	S	E	■	34 G	I	R	L	■	35 E	N	O	L
36 R	M	N	■	■	37 N	A	O	M	I	■	■	38 T	R	A
39 T	A	S	40 K	■	41 A	U	D	I	■	42 A	43 D	I	E	U
44 A	L	K	A	45 L	I	Z	E	■	46 O	T	H	E	R	S
■	■	■	47 D	I	V	E	■	48 B	L	E	U	■	■	■
49 S	50 A	51 D	D	L	E	■	52 B	E	D	■	53 R	54 I	55 L	56 E
57 A	L	I	I	■	58 T	59 O	R	A	H	■	60 R	B	I	S
61 M	I	S	S	■	62 E	L	E	N	A	■	63 I	A	M	S
64 E	A	C	H	■	■	65 A	L	O	T	■	66 E	R	N	E

CROSSWORD #7

1 S	2 W	3 A	4 M	5 I	■	6 C	7 A	8 A	9 N	■	10 L	11 A	12 C	13 K
14 P	E	C	A	N	■	15 I	M	R	E	■	16 A	L	A	N
17 E	A	R	N	S	■	18 R	I	C	O	■	19 R	I	C	E
20 C	R	E	A	T	21 U	R	E	■	22 L	23 E	G	A	T	E
■	■	■	24 T	I	T	I	■	25 M	I	T	O	S	I	S
26 O	27 N	28 S	A	L	E	■	29 B	A	T	H	■	■	■	■
30 R	O	A	R	■	31 P	32 U	R	C	H	A	33 S	34 E	35 R	36 S
37 I	T	S	M	38 E	■	39 P	O	R	■	40 N	A	D	I	R
41 G	A	S	S	T	42 A	T	I	O	43 N	■	44 G	A	L	A
■	■	■	■	45 A	W	O	L	■	46 C	47 H	I	M	E	S
48 M	49 O	50 I	51 S	T	E	N	■	52 W	A	I	T	■	■	■
53 U	N	L	E	S	S	■	54 S	H	A	T	T	55 E	56 R	57 S
58 L	E	I	A	■	59 O	60 G	E	E	■	61 M	A	L	E	S
62 E	T	A	L	■	63 M	A	M	A	■	64 A	T	E	I	N
65 S	O	D	S	■	66 E	D	I	T	■	67 N	E	E	D	S

CROSSWORD #8

1 A	2 S	3 E	4 C	■	5 G	6 U	7 A	8 V	9 A	■	10 Z	11 E	12 A	13 L
14 R	A	M	A	■	15 A	G	L	O	W	■	16 A	G	E	E
17 L	A	M	B	■	18 T	A	B	L	E	19 S	P	O	O	N
20 O	R	A	L	21 B	■	22 N	E	T	■	23 H	A	S	N	T
■	■	■	24 E	R	25 O	D	E	■	26 E	A	T	■	■	■
27 M	28 A	29 S	C	A	R	A	■	30 E	N	M	A	31 S	32 S	33 E
34 A	R	M	A	D	A	■	35 R	S	T	U	■	36 T	O	N
37 N	A	I	R	■	38 T	39 O	U	C	H	■	40 S	E	R	T
41 S	I	L	■	42 S	I	R	E	■	43 R	44 A	P	I	E	R
45 E	L	E	46 C	T	O	R	■	47 M	A	S	O	N	R	Y
■	■	■	48 R	A	N	■	49 P	A	L	E	R	■	■	■
50 H	51 O	52 N	E	Y	■	53 A	R	N	■	54 A	A	55 R	56 O	57 N
58 T	R	E	A	S	59 O	N	O	U	60 S	■	61 D	O	N	A
62 T	E	E	S	■	63 S	A	B	R	A	■	64 I	S	U	P
65 P	O	R	E	■	66 S	T	E	E	P	■	67 C	A	S	E

CROSSWORD #9

1 D	2 O	3 S	4 E	■	5 F	6 R	7 A	8 N	9 C	■	10 T	11 O	12 S	13 S
14 E	T	O	N	■	15 E	A	S	E	L	■	16 A	R	O	O
17 A	T	N	O	■	18 E	D	I	N	A	■	19 B	E	D	S
20 F	O	S	S	21 I	L	I	F	E	R	22 O	U	S	■	■
■	■	■	■	23 L	E	O	■	■	24 I	L	L	■	■	■
■	25 U	26 N	27 D	E	R	S	28 T	29 A	N	D	A	30 B	31 L	32 E
33 S	N	O	O	D	■	■	34 A	L	E	E	■	35 L	O	S
36 S	I	L	O	■	37 A	38 T	B	A	T	■	39 R	I	O	T
40 S	T	A	■	41 E	U	R	O	■	■	42 F	A	T	S	O
43 S	E	N	44 S	A	T	I	O	45 N	46 A	L	I	Z	E	■
■	■	■	47 O	S	O	■	■	48 E	N	E	■	■	■	■
■	■	49 P	S	Y	C	50 H	51 O	A	N	A	52 L	53 Y	54 Z	55 E
56 P	57 E	S	O	■	58 R	E	N	T	A	■	59 Y	E	A	N
60 E	S	S	O	■	61 A	R	E	E	L	■	62 R	A	N	T
63 A	T	T	N	■	64 T	E	A	R	S	■	65 A	R	E	S

CROSSWORD #10

1 O	2 A	3 T	4 E	5 S		6 A	7 T	8 H	9 O	10 S		11 S	12 S	13 R
14 W	O	R	T	H		15 P	A	E	A	N		16 N	A	E
17 E	L	I	H	U		18 I	M	A	R	I		19 A	N	E
				20 T	21 E	N	O	R		22 V	23 I	R	A	L
24 S	25 I	26 B	27 L	I	N	G			28 A	E	N	E	A	S
29 C	O	L	O	N	Y		30 H	31 A	L	L	S			
32 O	N	I	N		33 A	34 W	A	R	E		35 T	36 A	37 S	38 S
39 R	I	N	G			40 O	S	E			41 A	L	L	A
42 N	A	I	F		43 L	O	T	S	44 A		45 N	C	A	R
			46 A	47 B	O	D	E		48 T	49 A	C	O	M	A
50 S	51 N	52 O	C	A	T			53 U	N	L	E	A	S	H
54 L	O	R	E	N		55 A	56 R	R	O	W				
57 A	T	A		58 A	59 S	T	A	B		60 A	61 M	62 A	63 T	64 I
65 T	O	T		66 N	A	I	R	A		67 Y	E	S	E	S
68 E	N	E		69 A	S	P	E	N		70 S	A	K	E	R

CROSSWORD #11

1 S	2 L	3 E	4 D	■	5 B	6 R	7 A	8 S	9 S	■	10 T	11 S	12 P	13 S
14 W	E	R	E	■	15 R	A	N	T	O	■	16 E	A	R	L
17 E	E	L	S	■	18 E	I	D	E	R	■	19 E	V	O	E
■	20 R	E	P	21 R	E	S	E	N	T	22 A	T	I	V	E
■	■	■	23 O	O	Z	E	S	■	■	24 T	E	N	E	T
25 I	26 N	27 S	I	D	E	■	■	28 A	29 L	A	R	■	■	■
30 G	A	O	L	■	■	31 E	32 X	C	E	L	S	33 I	34 O	35 R
36 O	I	L	■	37 L	38 I	C	E	N	S	E	■	39 V	S	O
40 T	R	E	41 M	A	T	O	D	E	■	■	42 B	O	L	A
■	■	■	43 I	D	O	L	■	■	44 T	45 E	R	R	O	R
46 L	47 I	48 S	L	E	■	■	49 S	50 T	O	M	A	■	■	■
51 A	D	M	I	N	52 I	53 S	T	R	A	T	I	54 V	55 E	■
56 N	E	A	T	■	57 A	W	A	I	T	■	58 L	I	M	59 A
60 K	A	L	I	■	61 M	A	C	L	E	■	62 L	E	I	S
63 A	L	L	A	■	64 S	T	Y	L	E	■	65 E	S	T	E

CROSSWORD #12

1 S	2 C	3 A	4 N	■	■	■	5 A	6 F	7 T	■	8 S	9 L	10 O	11 G
12 T	O	L	E	13 T	■	14 B	A	B	A	■	15 T	O	T	E
16 O	M	A	N	I	■	17 T	R	I	P	■	18 I	O	T	A
19 A	B	S	E	N	20 T	E	E	■	21 E	22 E	R	I	E	R
■	■	■	■	23 T	O	N	■	24 E	S	T	■	25 E	R	S
26 M	27 E	28 R	29 C	E	R	■	30 S	A	T	U	31 P	■	■	■
32 A	L	O	U	D	■	33 R	E	T	R	I	E	34 V	35 A	36 L
37 S	L	I	T	■	38 F	O	A	M	Y	■	39 T	A	M	O
40 C	E	L	E	41 B	R	A	T	E	■	42 P	A	S	E	O
■	■	■	43 R	U	I	N	S	■	44 S	I	L	E	N	T
45 E	46 L	47 I	■	48 M	G	S	■	49 R	U	M	■	■	■	■
50 S	E	R	51 A	P	H	■	52 K	E	E	P	53 S	54 A	55 K	56 E
57 T	O	A	D	■	58 T	59 A	R	E	■	60 L	I	T	E	R
61 A	N	T	E	■	62 E	N	I	D	■	63 E	N	O	L	A
64 B	E	E	S	■	65 N	O	S	■	■	■	66 E	M	T	S

CROSSWORD #13

1 A	2 R	3 R	4 A	5 U	■	6 I	7 N	8 C	9 A	■	10 P	11 A	12 L	13 S
14 L	O	A	N	S	■	15 T	O	L	D	■	16 O	R	E	O
17 B	A	N	T	U	■	18 E	G	A	D	■	19 L	O	N	I
20 A	N	D	E	A	21 N	■	22 O	R	I	23 G	I	N	A	L
■	■	■	■	24 L	E	25 A	■	26 O	T	I	T	I	S	■
27 S	28 I	29 M	30 I	L	A	R	■	■	31 I	L	E	■	■	■
32 F	L	A	M	Y	■	33 E	34 N	35 R	O	L	■	36 C	37 P	38 R
39 P	E	R	P	■	40 S	W	O	O	N	■	41 A	A	R	E
42 D	D	E	■	43 V	I	E	W	S	■	44 A	L	L	O	T
■	■	■	45 S	E	C	■	■	46 E	47 B	B	T	I	D	E
■	48 S	49 P	A	R	K	50 Y	■	51 S	U	B	■	■	■	■
52 C	A	R	C	A	N	E	53 T	■	54 S	A	55 S	56 S	57 E	58 S
59 A	P	A	R	■	60 E	S	A	61 I	■	62 S	A	C	R	E
63 R	O	T	E	■	64 S	E	R	T	■	65 I	N	U	S	E
66 D	R	E	D	■	67 S	S	N	S	■	68 D	E	T	E	R

CROSSWORD #14

1 T	2 A	3 B	4 S	■	5 A	6 M	7 A	8 N	9 A	■	10 A	11 R	12 A	13 L
14 S	L	E	W	■	15 F	O	R	U	M	■	16 S	H	I	P
17 P	O	R	E	■	18 R	U	M	B	A	■	19 S	O	N	G
20 S	U	N	D	21 R	I	E	S	■	22 S	23 I	E	S	T	A
■	■	■	24 I	O	C	■	■	25 S	S	S	S	■	■	■
26 F	27 I	28 E	S	T	A	■	■	29 A	I	R	S	30 H	31 I	32 P
33 O	M	A	H	A	■	34 M	35 A	N	N	■	■	36 O	S	O
37 C	A	T	■	■	38 R	E	T	A	G	■	■	39 R	T	S
40 A	G	A	■	■	41 A	S	E	A	■	42 C	43 A	N	O	E
44 L	E	T	45 T	46 E	R	S	■	■	47 T	O	R	S	O	S
■	■	■	48 A	C	E	Y	■	■	49 A	I	M	■	■	■
50 S	51 E	52 C	T	O	R	■	53 H	54 I	S	T	O	55 R	56 I	57 C
58 H	A	U	T	■	59 I	60 D	E	S	T	■	61 I	O	N	A
62 O	R	E	O	■	63 P	E	R	L	E	■	64 R	U	N	E
65 E	N	D	O	■	66 E	A	S	E	D	■	67 E	T	O	N

CROSSWORD #15

1 W	2 A	3 T	4 E	5 R	6 M	7 A	8 N	■	9 S	10 H	11 A	12 S	13 T	14 A
15 E	D	E	N	T	A	T	E	■	16 R	O	T	T	E	N
17 R	E	N	D	E	R	E	D	■	18 S	O	N	A	N	T
19 E	N	S	■	20 S	O	I	■	■	■	21 T	O	R	A	H
22 N	O	I	23 R	■	24 O	N	25 E	26 D	27 G	E	■	28 E	N	E
29 T	I	T	I	30 A	N	■	31 R	O	A	N	■	32 A	T	M
■	33 D	Y	A	D	■	34 B	A	L	L	A	35 S	T	S	■
■	■	■	36 T	U	37 M	E	S	C	E	N	T	■	■	■
■	38 D	39 I	A	L	O	G	U	E	■	40 N	E	41 A	42 L	■
43 T	I	M	■	44 T	S	A	R	■	45 E	Y	E	L	E	46 T
47 U	V	A	■	48 E	S	T	E	49 E	M	■	50 L	A	V	A
51 S	U	G	52 A	R	■	■	■	53 N	O	54 V	■	55 M	E	L
56 C	L	I	M	A	57 X	■	58 M	E	T	A	59 M	E	R	E
60 A	G	N	A	T	E	■	61 G	R	E	N	A	D	E	S
62 N	E	E	D	E	D	■	63 M	O	D	E	R	A	T	E

CROSSWORD #16

1 S	2 E	3 G	4 A	5 L	■	6 R	7 A	8 N	9 T	10 S	■	11 S	12 D	13 I
14 S	T	A	R	E	■	15 I	D	I	O	T	■	16 H	U	D
17 R	A	I	S	E	■	18 C	O	A	T	I	■	19 I	C	Y
■	■	■	■	20 W	21 H	O	S	■	■	22 R	23 E	N	A	L
24 P	25 H	26 A	27 R	A	O	H	■	28 I	29 S	R	A	E	L	■
30 R	E	T	U	R	N	■	31 I	N	P	U	T	■	■	■
32 A	I	R	E	D	■	33 A	N	T	I	P	A	34 T	35 H	36 Y
37 T	R	A	■	■	38 E	L	L	E	N	■	■	39 R	O	E
40 E	S	S	41 E	42 N	T	I	A	L	■	43 C	44 H	A	R	M
■	■	■	45 R	E	N	E	W	■	46 F	A	M	I	N	E
■	47 T	48 A	I	W	A	N	■	49 M	O	I	S	T	E	N
50 Q	U	E	E	N	■	■	51 T	O	O	T	■	■	■	■
52 A	N	D	■	53 E	54 T	55 H	E	L	■	56 I	57 N	58 U	59 S	60 E
61 D	E	E	■	62 S	H	E	R	E	■	63 F	I	N	E	R
64 I	D	S	■	65 S	E	E	P	S	■	66 F	L	I	N	G

CROSSWORD #17

1 C	2 O	3 M	4 M	5 A	■	6 P	7 E	8 T	9 E	10 R	■	11 I	12 S	13 M
14 A	R	O	A	R	■	15 A	L	I	N	E	■	16 M	E	A
17 T	A	N	Y	A	■	18 R	I	C	E	P	19 A	P	E	R
20 S	L	O	■	21 B	22 O	S	S	■	■	23 L	E	E	R	S
■	■	24 P	25 R	I	C	E	■	26 B	27 E	A	R	I	S	H
28 A	29 F	L	O	A	T	■	30 A	B	A	C	O	■	■	■
31 Y	E	A	R	N	■	32 I	R	A	T	E	■	33 R	34 Y	35 A
36 E	E	N	Y	■	37 L	O	L	L	S	■	38 S	E	A	S
39 S	S	E	■	40 H	O	T	E	L	■	41 C	A	P	R	I
■	■	■	42 L	E	N	A	S	■	43 A	R	M	L	E	T
44 S	45 A	46 V	I	N	G	S	■	47 E	L	O	P	E	■	■
48 P	R	I	M	P	■	■	49 O	T	T	O	■	50 A	51 N	52 I
53 A	T	O	N	E	54 M	55 E	N	T	■	56 K	57 U	D	O	S
58 N	O	L	■	59 C	O	R	E	A	■	60 E	L	E	N	A
61 K	O	A	■	62 K	E	E	L	S	■	63 D	E	R	E	K

CROSSWORD #18

1 M	2 A	3 N	4 I	5 L	6 A		7 R	8 O	9 M		10 T	11 A	12 L	13 C
14 A	B	A	T	E	S		15 A	R	A		16 E	L	I	A
17 B	O	N	S	A	I		18 S	A	G		19 E	L	E	M
			20 A	F	F	21 E	C	T	I	22 O	N	A	T	E
23 R	24 A	25 L	L	Y		26 T	A	E		27 I	S	T	O	O
28 A	T	O	I		29 N	O	L		30 S	L	Y			
31 B	A	S	E	32 N	J	I		33 R	T	E		34 I	35 S	36 A
37 A	R	E		38 A	O	L		39 E	A	R		40 L	E	U
41 T	I	S		42 P	R	E		43 F	I	S	44 H	I	N	G
			45 R	I	D		46 M	I	D		47 E	A	S	E
48 E	49 S	50 T	E	E		51 I	A	L		52 E	I	D	E	R
53 D	I	S	G	R	54 U	N	T	L	55 I	N	G			
56 G	N	A	R		57 S	T	U		58 S	A	H	59 A	60 R	61 A
62 A	C	R	E		63 E	R	R		64 A	T	T	H	A	T
65 R	E	S	T		66 D	O	E		67 N	E	S	S	I	E

CROSSWORD #19

1 S	2 A	3 N	4 A	5 A	■	6 S	7 P	8 A	9 T	■	10 A	11 G	12 R	13 A
14 O	P	E	N	S	■	15 L	A	M	E	■	16 C	R	E	W
17 D	I	E	T	S	■	18 A	L	I	E	■	19 T	I	N	A
20 S	E	R	I	A	21 T	I	M	■	22 T	23 E	A	S	E	R
■	■	■	24 P	I	R	N	■	25 O	E	R	S	T	E	D
26 A	27 R	28 G	A	L	I	■	29 M	A	R	T	■	■	■	■
30 M	O	A	T	■	31 B	32 O	O	K	S	E	33 L	34 L	35 E	36 R
37 A	U	G	H	38 T	■	39 T	R	U	■	40 S	A	I	D	A
41 S	T	A	Y	A	42 T	H	O	M	43 E	■	44 B	R	E	T
■	■	■	■	45 K	E	E	N	■	46 S	47 L	O	A	N	E
48 P	49 I	50 O	51 N	E	E	R	■	52 T	S	A	R	■	■	■
53 R	O	D	E	N	T	■	54 P	R	E	M	I	55 E	56 R	57 E
58 O	N	O	R	■	59 H	60 O	N	E	■	61 B	O	W	E	R
62 B	I	R	D	■	63 E	L	I	A	■	64 D	U	E	T	S
65 E	A	S	Y	■	66 R	A	N	T	■	67 A	S	S	E	T

CROSSWORD #20

1 M	2 O	3 L	4 D	■	5 S	6 L	7 Y	8 L	9 Y	■	10 H	11 A	12 A	13 S
14 A	N	E	W	■	15 P	A	S	H	A	■	16 I	S	T	O
17 S	N	E	E	■	18 I	B	E	A	M	■	19 S	T	O	A
20 T	O	R	E	21 A	D	O	R	S	■	22 S	T	A	I	R
■	■	■	23 B	R	E	R	■	24 A	25 W	H	O	■	■	■
26 A	27 M	28 C	■	29 T	R	I	30 B	■	31 A	E	R	32 A	33 T	34 E
35 P	E	A	36 C	E	■	37 O	R	38 A	L	■	39 I	D	I	G
40 E	R	G	O	■	41 Q	U	A	C	K	■	42 A	L	E	E
43 A	G	E	R	■	44 A	S	I	A	■	45 S	N	A	G	S
46 K	E	Y	P	47 A	D	■	48 N	D	49 A	K	■	50 I	S	T
■	■	■	51 O	M	I	52 T	■	53 E	R	I	54 K	■	■	■
55 A	56 N	57 E	R	A	■	58 W	59 O	M	A	N	H	60 O	61 O	62 D
63 D	O	L	E	■	64 S	E	D	E	R	■	65 M	O	N	A
66 A	N	K	A	■	67 R	A	I	S	A	■	68 E	N	T	R
69 R	E	E	L	■	70 S	K	E	E	T	■	71 R	A	V	E

About The Author

Jason Scotts has quite a number of interests and over the years he has taken a special interest in memory and the ways that it can be improved. The seed of interest was planted when he was trying to find his own way to remember his own work for exams. That was when he started to delve into the world of memory exercises to try and find the best one to help him to achieve his goals.

From the success that he had he made the decision to put together his own set of texts to explain to the various things that can be done to improve various aspects of memory to the interested reader.

Jason is aware from his own experience that it will not be as easy as it seems in the first instances and he makes this clear in his texts. It is a process that has to be done in phases and before you know it your memory will be up to par.